Fishing Washington's
ENDLESS SEASON

A Guide to Year 'Round Fishing

Steve Probasco

Flying Pencil Publications
Scappoose, Oregon

Published by Flying Pencil Publications in collaboration with Four Rivers Press. Maps in this book are for planning reference only, not for navigation. Flying Pencil Publications, Four Rivers Press, and the author shall have no liability or responsibility with respect to physical harm, property damage, or any other loss or damage asserted to be caused directly or indirectly by the information in this book.

To receive our catalog of Northwest fishing books, write or call:
Flying Pencil Publications
33126 SW Callahan Road
Scappoose, Oregon 97056
(503) 543-7171 FAX (503) 543-7172

Photographs by Steve Probasco. Maps by Madelynne Sheehan. Cover and decorative art by August Kristoferson. Technical illustrations by Kari Valley. Cover design by John Laursen.

Printed in the United States of America.

10 9 8 7 6 5 4 3 2 1

Library of Congress Catalog Card Number: 97-061614

ISBN: 0-916473-12-0

To Cecil Probasco, my dad, who taught me early in life the joy of fishing and the love of the outdoors.

Acknowledgments

A special thanks to Maddy Sheehan for her tolerance, encouragement, and editing, and to my fishing partners for their companionship and willingness to help out with photography. I would also like to thank everyone who, somewhere along the line, may have given me a tidbit of information about their favorite fishin' hole or special place.

Also by Steve Probasco

Fly Patterns for the Pacific Northwest
River Journal: Yakima River
River Journal: Big Hole
Fy Fishing Desert & High Arid Lakes
The Art of Fly Tying

Other Titles from Flying Pencil

Fishing in Oregon, by Madelynne Sheehan
Fishing in Oregon's Endless Season, by Scott Richmond
Fishing in Oregon's Cascade Lakes, by Scott Richmond
Fishing in Oregon's Deschutes River, by Scott Richmond

Contents

Winter

Winter Steelhead

Trout and Panfish for the Hardy

Puget Sound Resident Salmon

Whitefish

Maps

LEGEND

- - - - - - - -	trail or track	⊿	boat access
ı ı ı ı ı ı ı ı	railroad	Λ	campground
————	secondary road	◯	county or state road
————	major road	⬠	U.S. highway
～～～	creek	⬯	interstate highway
🗘 marsh	marsh	▭	forest road
░░ tidal flat	tidal flat	🥃	national forest road
～～➤ streamflow	current		

Preface

As a kid growing up in Ellensburg, in central Washington, my first fishing experiences were on little farm creeks where my worms and grasshoppers found their way into the mouths of many hungry, willing trout. My dad took me fishing on spring weekends, and during summer vacations I fished these streams on my own almost every day, limited only by how far I was willing to bicycle.

Then one day a school friend, Arn, invited me to fish a little bluegill pond outside of town. He told me stories of catching 100 fish a day. I didn't believe him.

The next day, his dad dropped us off at the pond, and we dangled worms in the "seaweed," yanking out bluegills right and left. I discovered a new fishery, and Arn and I were inseparable for a summer. But Arn moved away, and I moved on—to fly fishing.

While most kids spent their allowances on movies, candy, or airplane models, I bought Dan Bailey flies at the local sporting goods store. I generally maintained a collection of six flies: three mosquitoes and three Royal Coachmen. That's all I needed.

I knew nothing about fly fishing when I started, and I had no teacher. I read books and taught myself. I admired those "rich" people on TV who fished far off places like Canada and Alaska, and I ached to live a life like theirs.

Meanwhile, back on the farm, I discovered that when my fly floated naturally along a grassy bank, the trout would sip it in. If my leader caught the current and the fly skated, the fish would ignore it. I grew to love fly fishing, and my little bait rod gathered dust in the garage. I was a fly fisherman now.

For Christmas one year, my mom and dad gave me a fly tying kit. I spent countless hours devising hideous creations, but eventually I tied a fly that I felt would actually fool a fish. It was a Carey Special.

When trout season opened in April, my dad took me out to one of our favorite streams. It was a cold, windy day, but I was determined to fish my own flies. Dad was catching trout right and left on worms, but I stuck with it and eventually hooked a trout. I still remember the feeling of intense satisfaction.

As the summers passed, I fished bigger and bigger waters and hooked fish that dwarfed the little stream trout of my youth. Fly fishing remained my passion, but I became less of a fly fishing purist, returning to some of my earlier techniques and learning others as weather, water, good sense, and the capabilities and interests of my own youngsters dictated.

Over the past thirty-five years, Washington has revealed its fishing treasures to me—the glorious Yakima, Puget Sound, the Columbia, rich desert lakes, eager alpine trout, salmon, the off-shore fisheries, steelhead. One of the most important things I learned is that I don't have to wait for "the season" to open in order to go fishing. Washington has an endless fishing season, if we're willing to open our minds to different techniques, explore new fisheries, and wear a little rubber off our tires.

Fishing Washington's Endless Season is not an inclusive guide to the state's fishing. Rather, it is one angler's selection of favorite places and fisheries. It is organized by seasons and (roughly) by month to illustrate the kinds of choices we in Washington can make as we move through the calendar year. (In truth, most of the species I write about can be taken in more than one season, as I try to point out in my essays.)

I hope this collection will serve as a starting point for anglers new to Washington and who are overwhelmed by the choices it offers. I hope it will serve as inspiration for anglers ready to expand their fishing horizons. And I hope it will entertain and awaken the memories of long-time anglers who—like me—have responded to the lure of Washington's endless season and are hopelessly hooked. Good fishing to us all!

Steve Probasco
Raymond, WA

Spring

The Wynoochee was at its maximum fishable level, and its color was right on the edge. When the sun broke through thick clouds and a shaft of light struck the alders on the far bank, I noticed that the spindly trees were beginning to bud and that streamside willows were greening up. I made a few half-hearted casts and decided to call it a season.

Winter steelheading had been good; many fish had come to hand. But now, snow melt and incessant rains were knocking the rivers out of shape. By the time this stream dropped back to optimum level, it would be closed to steelheading.

Of course, other steelhead rivers—the Hoh, the Skagit—were just hitting their prime. In Washington state, steelhead can be found and fished in some river every month of the year. But I'd had enough for the time being. I needed a break from the cold and wet.

As I walked the muddy trail back to my car, I pondered, *What next?* A Washington spring offers anglers many choices. Besides the steelhead still available in Puget Sound tributaries and some coastal rivers, bottomfish grow active off the coast, spring chinook begin heading upstream, and bass shake themselves out of winter lethargy. But for me, when the weather begins to warm, it is the thought of eastside trout that first stirs my blood.

It's true that a number of lakes east of the Cascades are open year 'round, but lake fishing is generally slow until March 1, when a bunch more eastside lakes open for trout. It's also true that, in Washington, spring comes first to the westside (west of the Cascade Mountains), while the eastside (all points east of the Cascades) can still feel a lot like winter, though both eastside and westside trout fishing opportunities pick up about the same time.

My personal eastside favorites are the lakes of the Columbia Basin in Central Washington. There's probably equally good lake fishing farther east, but my car seems to have a mind of its own and rarely makes it past the turn-offs to Quail and Lenore lakes. Quail is open year 'round, Lenore opens March 1, and Dry Falls Lake (another spring favorite) opens with the general trout opener the last Saturday in April.

Slipping and sliding along the muddy trail leading away from the Wynoochee, my mental gears were turning. By the time I reached the car and got the heater going, I had pretty much made up my mind to head east. I'd get a little sagebrush and trout into my system, then I'd begin thinking about the weeks ahead. As always, I knew I would fish spring for all it was worth.

Desert Trout

Lake Lenore, late March

The wind was exceptional, even for eastern Washington. By the time we arrived in mid-afternoon, all boats and all but one daredevil float tuber had abandoned the water. With whitecaps rolling across its surface, Lenore, looked more like the Pacific Ocean on a miserable day than an inland lake in spring.

The lone tuber teetered on a wave crest, then a strong gust caught his tube from the bottom and tossed him ten feet through the air before he touched down—upside down. He clung to his tube and kicked to shore. Yes, the wind can blow in eastern Washington, especially in spring!

That was the beginning and end of our fishing trip, but as we headed back across the mountains, we made plans to return. Even though spring weather is unpredictable in eastern Washington, trout fishing is unquestionably best east of the Cascades, where warmer summer temperatures foster abundant aquatic weed and insect growth, which in turn grow big trout. We were far from discouraged.

The following weekend, the weather forecast looked good, and when we pulled into the first public access at the south end of the lake, we were pleased to see a calm Lake Lenore shimmering in the early morning sun.

As we blew up our float tubes, other anglers were already working the shorelines from tubes and small cartop boats. Several were playing fish at the same time, not unusual during this time of year when Lenore's Lahontan cutthroat are schooled for their pre-spawn ritual. I fumbled pump and gear more than once in my eagerness to get out on the water.

Lenore's weed line extends about 20 feet from shore. Although trout cruise around in this jungle, it is difficult to fish. So we kicked our tubes just beyond it and cast brightly colored Woolly Buggers and smaller nymphs towards the weeds, stripping them slowly back to our positions.

Lenore lived up to our expectations that day. Our casts met with hookup after hookup, and by mid-afternoon we were exhausted and (for the time being) replete.

It only takes a few sunny days to turn on eastern Washington lake fishing. By the time it opens for trout fishing March 1, Lake Lenore is often at its best. Located just to the north of the town of Soap Lake, Lenore is a shallow 1,700 acres and hosts a fishery that is relatively new to the Pacific Northwest.

Despite attempted stockings with a variety of species, Lenore's waters were too alkaline to sustain trout until the introduction of Lahontan cutthroat in 1977. The first Lahontans came from Nevada's Carson River-Heenan Lake strain. Thirty trout were placed in live boxes in the lake. The fish adapted well to the alkaline water, and in 1979 another 35,000 fry were planted. In 1980, 135,000 more fry were stocked. Today, Lake Lenore hosts a healthy, self-perpetuating population of these powerful cutthroat.

Lake Lenore is one of my favorite places to take beginning trout anglers or float tubers. On most visits, getting into fish is not a problem, and there is no better way to put the bug into beginners. This is where I introduced my own boys to lake fishing.

On that day a half-dozen or so years ago, I rigged up the boys' rods with six-pound tippet and hot-colored, flashy Woolly Buggers. I showed them how to kick out in their float tubes and suggested they work slowly along the weed line about thirty feet from shore. Both Luke and Jordan were into three-pound trout (average here!) within a few minutes. I don't know how many fish we hooked and released that day, but the number was significant, and our success became something of a problem. As their fishing careers progressed, the boys used that first outing at Lake Lenore as the base-

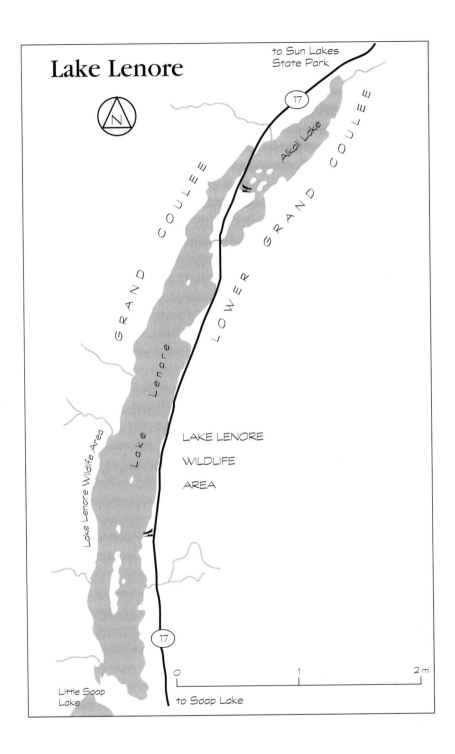

Lake Lenore

to Sun Lakes
State Park

17

Alkali Lake

GRAND COULEE

LOWER GRAND COULEE

Lake Lenore

Lake Lenore Wildlife Area

LAKE LENORE

WILDLIFE

AREA

17

0   1   2 mi

Little Soap
Lake

to Soap Lake

Selective Fishery Regulations on Lake Lenore increase the size of the average catch.

line for judging all subsequent lakes and fishing trips. Few could stand up to the comparison!

Most fly anglers at Lenore target the big Lahontans with flashy flies like orange Woolly Buggers and brightly colored Carey Specials. However, there is a tremendous population of *Callibaetis* mayflies here. A size 12 Gold Ribbed Hares Ear Nymph on a sink-tip line will consistently produce better for me than any other pattern, flashy or otherwise, especially during spring.

State Highway 17 follows Lenore's eastern shore, and there are several wide spots in the road with ample room to park a few cars. Float tubers can launch at most of these spots. There are public boat ramps near the north and south ends of the lake.

When fishing close to the road, you will often see cars slow down and even stop along the highway so the anglers inside can get a better view. If you get a fish on, you may see the car doors fly open and their occupants race to the trunk to retrieve fishing gear!

It's tough to fly fish from the highway bank because the steep rock slope limits back-casting. But with spinning gear you can easily work the whole eastern shoreline, and the Lahontans are just as eager to take a spinner or spoon as they are a fly.

For spin fishing, most anglers prefer small, brightly colored spinners and spoons. A light- to medium-weight spinning rod makes for quite a battle with a three- or four-pound cutthroat.

Trolling is also effective. Using the same types of spinners and spoons, troll just outside the weedline, about thirty feet from shore, and follow the shoreline.

Keep in mind that Lake Lenore falls under the Selective Fishery Regulations of the Washington Department of Fish and Wildlife (WDFW), which state that anglers must use artificial flies or lures with single, barbless hooks. Internal combustion engines are not allowed, so trolling is limited to small electric motors, oars, or fins.

These regulations are responsible for the quality trout fishing in Lenore and many other central Washington lakes. A few years back, while still open for year 'round angling with a one-fish limit, Lake Lenore took a downward turn. At that time, a good number of cutthroat were approaching the ten-pound range. In spring when the trout migrated towards the lake ends to spawn, many anglers concentrated on these areas, fishing till they caught a trophy-size trout, which they usually dispatched on the spot. Ice fishing during the winter also depleted the population of mature trout. After a few years, the numbers of large fish hooked began to decline.

WDFW jumped on the problem with a regulation change that requires catch-and-release fishing when the majority of the fish are concentrated at the lake ends from March 1 to May 31. From June 1 to November 30, there is a one-fish limit. Lenore is now closed during the winter.

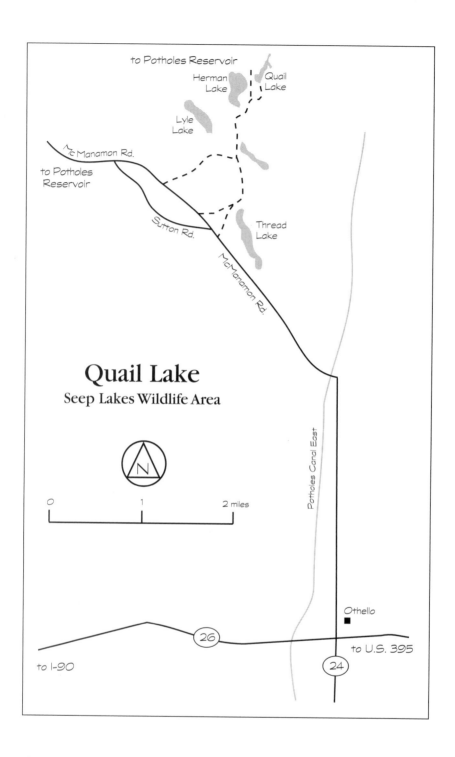

to Potholes Reservoir

Herman
Lake

Quail
Lake

Lyle
Lake

McManamon Rd.

to Potholes
Reservoir

Sutton Rd.

Thread
Lake

McManamon Rd.

Quail Lake
Seep Lakes Wildlife Area

N

0   1   2 miles

Potholes Canal East

Othello

26

to U.S. 395

to I-90

24

Quail Lake, early April

The pungent smell of sage filled the air as I walked the half-mile trail to the lake. A few months from now, the soft green grasses and wildflowers that covered the ground would be baked golden by the sun, accompanied by blowing dust and temperatures upwards of 100°F. But tromping through the desert at this time of year can be rewarding for a Washington trout angler. My destination this day was Quail Lake, one of my favorite spring fisheries.

Quail is south of Potholes Reservoir in an area known as "the seep lakes" or just "the seeps." This region is part of the great Columbia Plateau, one of the largest basaltic lava flows in the world, covering approximately 50,000 square miles.

The seeps were created when Potholes Reservoir filled following the completion of O'Sullivan Dam. The downward pressure of 125,000 acres of water forced ground water through the area's subterranean network of volcanic fissures and channels, extruding it into small canyons and valleys for many miles south of the reservoir. There are more than 70 seep lakes. (See map p. 160.) Today, a good number of the seeps contain trout.

The largest trout I ever took from a public water in the state of Washington came from Quail Lake. In fact, on the day I took that big rainbow, I saw other several other anglers take fish of the same caliber.

Like many of the seeps, Quail is heavily vegetated, hosting prolific insect hatches and fast-growing fish. Its smaller trout, those 15 inches and under, look like footballs, with little heads and fat bellies.

These trout are planted, as are most seep lake fish, since the seeps offer little spawning habitat in the form of inlet or outlet streams. The average size of seep lake trout varies depending on the number of trout introduced into a lake and the frequency with which they are planted. Another factor determining average size of the catch is the number of fish taken from the water by anglers. The best seep lakes, like Quail, are fly-fishing-only, with catch-and-release the rule. These regulations allow many trout to grow to maturity. In such fertile waters, "maturity" means "really big."

On the day of my big trout, we were casting black Woolly Buggers along the weedbeds and stripping them back slowly. The water was only five or six feet deep, and with a sinking-tip line and short, four-foot leader tapered to 3X, our flies seemed to stay right in the feeding zone of those big cruisers. I really don't think there is a fly that can match the fish catching capabilities of the Woolly Bugger. If there is, I haven't found it!

Since Quail is open all year, it is one of the best waters to hit in early spring, as soon as the water warms enough to stimulate hatches. The first hatch at Quail is the *Chironomid* (midge). Midges are a mainstay in the diet of stillwater trout, and they are incredibly abundant in Washington's desert lakes in early spring.

The pupal stage of the midge is the most valuable to the trout fly angler. At times, the surface of a lake will be covered with trout rising to take midge pupae near the surface, dotting the water with rings that look like raindrops.

Midges come in a variety of colors, including black, brown, olive, and tan. Imitations can be fished from the top to the bottom at any hour of the day, and there are those who will do just that. But the naturals are most vulnerable just as they reach the surface, where the adult emerges from the pupal husk. This can take place all day long during the spring, but as the water warms, hatches will be concentrated in mornings and evenings.

If midges are hatching in significant numbers, you will see the pupal husks floating on the water. In fact, if you are observant, you will witness the adults emerging from the split husks. Pay careful attention to the size and color of the husk, and choose an imitation that closely matches it. When I can't match the exact color, I try to at least match the size of the naturals, on the generally accepted theory that size is more important than color.

Where the trout have been heavily fished over, I usually use a 12- or 14-foot leader with about four feet of 5X tippet—6X if my flies

Tying the V-Rib Chironomid Pupa

Hook: Daiichi 1150, sizes 10 to 16

Thread: Black

Abdomen: Black V-Rib

Wingcase: Black Swiss Straw

Thorax: Black dubbing

Gills: White Poly Pro yarn

Step 1: Secure a piece of black V-Rib to the hook shank and wind forward two-thirds of the way up the hook shank.

Step 2: Tie in a piece of black Swiss Straw to be used later for the wingcase.

Step 3: Dub on a thorax of black dubbing. Make sure the thorax is about twice the thickness of the abdomen.

Step 4: Place a small section of Poly Pro yarn across the top of the hook in front of the thorax and secure with a figure eight motion of the tying thread.

Step 5: Pull Swiss Straw forward and secure at the head. Trim the Poly yarn so that it extends out only one-sixteenth of an inch on each side of the fly. Finish head, and cement to complete the V-Rib Chironomid Pupa.

Note: This fly should be tied in various colors to match the naturals found in any given water.

are met with refusals. You will seldom need a longer or finer leader when fishing a seep lake.

I rarely bother to fish midges unless I see the telltale raindrop rings. When I do, I fish the imitation in the surface film, since this is where trout are most likely to attack it. To fish the film, grease your leader with fly floatant to within an inch of the fly. This will let the fly sink slightly, looking very much like the natural pupa as it reaches the surface. Cast to the rises, then let the fly sit motionless, keeping a close eye on the floating leader, especially at the point where it draws under the surface near the fly. If the leader pulls under sharply, or does anything at all suspicious, raise your rod tip slightly. That's usually all it takes to set the hook.

Dry Falls Lake, late April

The sky was gray, and a light drizzle kept the windshield wipers slapping as we turned off State Highway 17 and wound down the hill to Sun Lakes State Park. Big cottonwoods swayed in the breeze. Canadian honkers waddled across  the road in front of our car. A couple of rough miles over a primitive road brought us to the Dry Falls parking lot. The view was magnificent, and there were only a couple of other cars there. It was my first visit to Dry Falls Lake.

Although I'd grown up in eastern Washington, I had never fly fished any of its quality lakes. I made my virgin trip with Garry Sandstrom. Garry now owns the Morning Hatch Fly Shoppe in Tacoma. But in those days we were just a couple of callow youths, newly hooked on fly fishing, who had met by chance in Raymond, where I lived. Garry had fished Dry Falls, and his tales of wily rainbows and stubborn browns whetted my appetite and resulted in this trip.

This was in the days before float tubes were popular. We set out in one-man rafts, heading for an area of the lake where there were

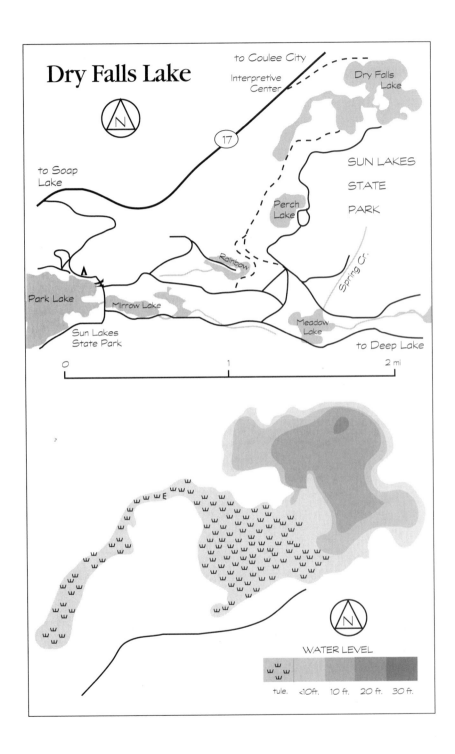

Dry Falls Lake

to Coulee City
Interpretive Center
Dry Falls Lake
17
to Soap Lake
SUN LAKES STATE PARK
Perch Lake
Spring Cr.
Rainbow
Park Lake
Mirrow Lake
Meadow Lake
Sun Lakes State Park
to Deep Lake

0   1   2 mi

WATER LEVEL

tule.   <10ft.   10 ft.   20 ft.   30 ft.

Float Tube Etiquette

The growing popularity of stillwater fishing in the northwest, and of float tubes in particular, has created a new set of problems at some lakes, Dry Falls included. Most of the problems could be easily solved if anglers would exercise a little common sense and consideration.

For example, float tubers who kick into the shallows in search of fish often kick up the bottom muck with their fins. This damages habitat for both insects and fish, and a band of clouded water drifts into the path of other anglers.

To avoid kicking up the muck when tubing, stay in deeper water at the edge of the shallows, and cast toward the weedbeds. Avoid kicking through areas where others are casting.

shallow, reedy rock piles on which we could stand and cast. On that silent morning, Garry and I cast small nymphs on sink-tip lines to dozens of eager trout. And I lost my heart to Dry Falls Lake.

Dry Falls and the surrounding area were formed by a receding glacier at the end of the last ice age. A few thousand years ago, the mighty Columbia River flowed over the vertical cliffs that surround this lake, creating a cataract many times greater than Niagara. Centuries of erosion have further sculpted the terrain into a panorama of lakes and towering cliffs.

Dry Falls is my favorite lake in the world. I love it for its sheer beauty and, not incidentally, for its trout. I have caught more rainbows and browns here than in any other lake in the state. But then, I spend a lot of time here.

The northern half of Dry Falls, below the cliffs, reaches a depth of 30 feet. The southern half is shallow and covered with aquatic plants. In spring and fall (as well as on cool summer mornings and evenings), you will find trout in these shallows. Nearly every stillwater aquatic insect flourishes here— dragonflies, damselflies, mayflies, midges. The shallows are a virtual insect smorgasbord.

If the afternoon sun gets to be too much for the trout, they head for the deeper half of the lake. Dry Falls is one of those lakes where you can successfully fish all day throughout the open season simply by changing techniques and locations.

I like to have two fly rods set up when I'm fishing Dry Falls, one with a floating fly line and the other with a full sinker, just to cover all bases. Of course it's only legal to fish with one rod at a time, but it's okay to carry a spare in Washington, and it's handy to have that other rod ready to go if you need to change tactics.

There are times when adult midges and *Callibaetis* mayflies are important, and you should have some of these patterns with you. But more often than not, sunken flies take the most fish. A short list of my favorite spring flies for Dry Falls includes: Gold Ribbed Hares Ear Nymph, Zug Bug, Black Woolly Bugger, Olive Woolly Worm, V-Rib Chironomid Pupa, Superfloss Chironomid Pupa, and Marabou Damsel.

Like most lakes in eastern Washington, the wind is a factor in spring. But Dry Falls is somewhat sheltered beneath its cliffs, and I have never seen it too windy to fish. Too windy to cast elegantly, but not too windy to fish!

I once had a photo assignment with a big New York magazine to get some shots of light-tackle spinning rods and trout on a western lake. Naturally, I chose Dry Falls for my shooting location. Since Selective Fishery Regulations apply here, I made sure I took only small spinners and spoons with single barbless hooks. I had never fished Dry Falls with spinning gear before, but that afternoon my little ultralight spinning outfit (spooled with two-pound test line) got a workout!

You really can't fish Dry Falls from the shore. Reeds and marshy ground prevent access except in a very few places. Float tubes are by far the most popular craft here, but small cartop boats, canoes, and personal boats work well, too. As in most Selective Fishery lakes, motors of all kinds are prohibited.

When I first fished Dry Falls with Garry Sandstrom, there were few anglers on the lake. These days, crowding can be a problem here and at other well-publicized eastside lakes, especially during the early season. Fortunately, there are a multitude of lakes in eastern Washington, many of which are virtually unknown. As a general rule, those without special regulations are often less crowded. Use USGS topo maps of the area to discover your own personal favorites. Though not all the seeps contain trout, you'll never know until you check them out!

Most of my spring trout fishing is done in the desert lakes of central Washington not because these are necessarily the best, but because they're the closest to my home. Lenice, Nunnally and Merry Lakes, in the Crab Creek Wildlife Area near the community of Beverly, are also among my favorites. Each of these lakes requires a half-mile hike in, but the walk is well worth the effort. All are shallow with prolific hatches and fisheries similar to that of Dry Falls.

Grimes Lake is a Lahontan cutthroat fishery near popular Jameson Lake. Both can be reached via the Jameson Lake Road, which cuts off Highway 2 just west of Dry Falls junction, the junction of highways 2 and 17. The largest Lahontan cutthroat I ever caught came from Grimes.

To the east, along Interstate 90 near the town of Sprague, lies Sprague Lake. To the north, in the foothills outside of Oroville, check out Chopaka Lake, possibly the best dry fly lake in the state. Further east, there are many good trout lakes in the Spokane area, including Silver and West Medical.

One could spend the entire spring fishing the trout lakes of eastern Washington and never fish the same lake twice.

Westside Trout Lakes

Merrill Lake, early April

A couple of days before, when we were tying flies around the warmth of the wood stove, a trip to Merrill Lake seemed like a good idea. My friends and I had been suffering from cabin fever. We needed a trout trip, but none of us had time to make the trek to our favorite fisheries in eastern Washington. But when we finally launched our float tubes and kicked our way through the mist on a chilly April morning, we were having second thoughts. We were cold, and although some midges were hatching, there was no sign of trout.

On the other hand, we had the place all to ourselves.

Merrill is a 344-acre fly-fishing-only lake southwest of Mt. St. Helens. It has drawn a lot of attention in recent years for its big *Hexagenia limbata* mayflies which hatch in July and August. There were also reports of 20-inch brown trout. Since Merrill is open the year 'round, it offers an enticing westside option in spring. But today's cold drizzle had given us an exclusive.

We started fishing on the east side of the lake near the campground. Working our way across in an attempt to warm up, we noticed a small cove and headed there. As we drew closer I saw a swirl in the water, then another. Trout were feeding, probably on midge pupae in the surface film.

When we reached the cove, I could see why the fish were there. The water was shallow with a weedy bottom, so it was warmer, and therefore attractive to aquatic insects and the trout that eat them.

We tied the midges to our tippets and cast across the cove in concert. As if following a director's baton, fish rose to each of our flies.

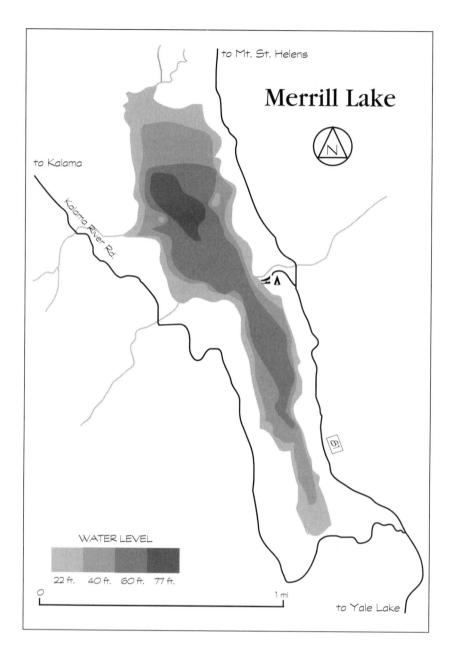

Catching trout that morning didn't surprise me, but their size did. Most were fat brown trout in the 16-to 20-inch range. I hadn't known western Washington could produce trout of this magnitude.

Before day's end, we had also taken a few smaller rainbows and cutthroat, but the big browns stole the show. Fishing held up through the midge hatch, then shut off cold. We switched to sinking lines and dredged the bottom with Woolly Buggers, but to no avail.

Subsequent trips to Merrill Lake have confirmed the pattern. When a hatch is on, the action is hot and heavy. When the hatch is over, it's hard to get a fish interested in any fly. This is not characteristic of western Washington lakes, but there is general agreement among anglers that Merrill is peculiar in this regard.

To get to Merrill, take Highway 503 west from Cougar, then follow FS Road 81 a few miles to the lake. You can also get there by following the Kalama River Road (gravel most of the way) from I-5 near the town of Kalama. The '96 flood buried the lake's boat ramp under a few feet of gravel and limited vehicle access to within one-eighth mile of the lake shore. Check with WDFW for updates on restoration.

Nearby Yale, Merwin, and Swift Creek reservoirs are also good producers of large trout, but they are too cold for much early season success.

Riffe Lake, early April

It was one of the most miserable spring mornings I had ever seen. But I had a new float tube, and I wanted to try it out. I exited Highway 12 at the east end of Riffe Lake, a 23-mile long reservoir on the Cowlitz River, and turned onto Kosmos Road. Driving, almost horizontal rain turned to equally ferocious hail. By the time I reached the lake, the ground was white.

A single fisherman huddled by a fire, sipping hot coffee. A giant pot sat brewing in the coals. I'm sure he thought I was nuts when I pulled my float tube out and started pumping it up.

After my gear was assembled, I walked over to visit a minute before taking the plunge. As I approached, he jumped up and ran over to his bobbing rod, which was propped up by a forked stick. A short battle produced a bright, chunky landlocked coho of about 14 inches, which he placed along with a couple others by his little driftwood shelter.

We engaged in some small talk, mostly me asking about the lake's fishing. Since this was my first trip to Riffe, I was eager to get all the information I could.

I learned that Riffe hosts several species, including landlocked coho salmon, rainbow trout, brown trout, small and largemouth bass, black crappie and bluegill. On this spring morning, it was the coho that were falling for this angler's corn nibblets, which he fished about 30 feet from shore on a basic bobber set-up.

I felt a little silly and looked anything but dignified as I waddled backwards into the water, holding my float tube around my middle, slipping and sliding on the hail covered rocks.

Once I got my rhythm down, finning against the wind wasn't too bad, and I was able to let out my sinking fly line and start a slow troll along the shoreline. I was using a small, nondescript streamer on a size 10 hook. After an hour, I was still fishless while my new friend on the bank had landed at least three more fish.

I gave it another hour, whipped by the wind and stung by intermittent hail, then hauled my numbed body out to beg a place by the fire. We resumed our conversation, and I learned that the best bass fishing on the lake takes place in spring when the water is up into the brush around the shorelines. Casting towards the brush from a boat is the way to approach these fish. I also learned that some very big trout are taken by trolling with flashers and spoons. Good spots for bank angling for landlocked coho are along the northeast shore where we were fishing, and at the Cowlitz River inlet.

Open year 'round, Riffe Lake offers a good cure for early spring

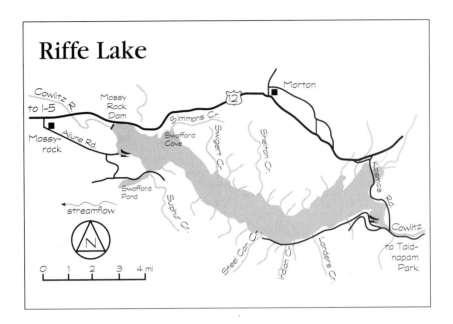

Riffe Lake

Cowlitz R.
to I-5

Mossy Rock Dam

Mossy-rock

Allune Rd.

Simmons Cr.

Swofford Cove

Swigert Cr.

Sherton Cr.

Morton

12

Kosmos Rd.

Cowlitz

to Taid-napam Park

Swofford Pond

Sulphur Cr.

Steel Con Cr.

Indian Cr.

Landers Cr.

streamflow

N

0 1 2 3 4 mi

fever. And with the variety of fish found in this water, there is something for just about every angling appetite.

There are parks with boat launches at each end of the lake. Once, while scouting the area, I saw a couple of anglers at the west end come in with two giant rainbows of five or six pounds each. The fish had been taken by trolling large spoons deep along the southern shore.

Other spring fishing possibilities in the Riffe Lake area include Swofford Pond and Mayfield Lake. Swofford is near the southwest corner of Riffe, separated only by a road. This 240-acre lake was formerly used for rearing steelhead. In recent years it has been stocked with bass, rainbows, brown trout, bluegill, and channel catfish. An old creek channel running through the little lake is a good place to look for lunker bass.

To reach Swofford Pond by vehicle, follow Swofford Road five miles from the town of Mossyrock. There is a boat ramp on the east end of the lake, but internal combustion engines are prohibited.

Mayfield Lake, just off Highway 12, offers an unusual fishery for tiger muskies as well as rainbows, landlocked coho, and a few smallmouth bass.

Tiger muskies are a sterile hybrid cross between a male northern pike and a female muskellunge. They were introduced into this 13-mile long reservoir in 1988 to help control the lake's huge squawfish and sucker population. Many of the tiger muskies are well over the legal minimum size of 36 inches and are taken by anglers fishing the weedbeds along the shoreline.

Neah Bay, gateway to some of Washington's best saltwater fishing.

Plump brown trout frequently steal the show at Merrill Lake.

Grimes is one of many desert lakes that offer good spring fishing.

Tim Irish with a Lahontan cutthroat.

Spring Chinook

Cowlitz River, April

The only thing I object to about fishing for spring chinook is, as my uncle "Pappy" would say, "you have to get up before breakfast!" You can't get up at dawn to go fishing; you have to be *fishing* at dawn. And when you live two hours from the river as I do, this makes for an early rise. Nevertheless, I have been known to make the supreme sacrifice to fish for spring chinook (springers) on the Cowlitz.

One of my most memorable springer experiences was several years ago. It was typical April weather, nasty and cold. There was just enough wind to make the little 12-foot aluminum boat hard to control, and more than enough wind to cut through our clothes and make us miserable.

We were in a line-up of four or five boats chugging along on a slow troll, working our way downriver towards the mouth of the Cowlitz. We had been trolling for a half hour or so without a bump. With each gust of wind, I thought of my warm bed back home and cursed the weather.

As we drew closer to the mouth, we saw several boats anchored right at the Columbia River confluence. When we got close enough for a good look, we saw a couple of bent rods and a flurry of nets being dipped over the side. Chattering teeth and numbed fingers were forgotten.

As I watched a fish being netted in front of us, my own rod tip slammed down, and I too had a fish on.

Spring chinook are incredibly powerful fighters. Fresh from the ocean, they have a far greater store of energy than do chinook which enter the river later in the season.

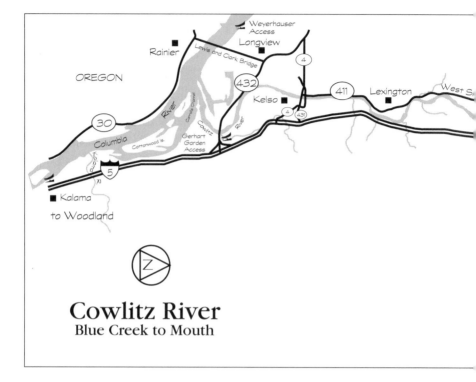

Cowlitz River
Blue Creek to Mouth

The fish I'd hooked seemed to be no exception. It ran a dangerous distance away from our boat, and I had an all out tug-of-war to get it back. From the fight, I was sure this was at least a 24-pounder, but when it finally came to net, it was half that size.

The amount of time a chinook feeds in the ocean determines its size. My 12-pounder had probably foraged the ocean for three years. A four-year fish would weigh 15 to 20 pounds, and a five-year fish might reach 30 pounds or more.

After landing my salmon, we headed back the way we came, making several passes up and down. Each time we returned to the mouth, we hoped one of the anchored boats might have headed home, but they never budged. Late comers—those of us who put in at daybreak—would have to take seconds.

Seconds wasn't bad, though, and we caught our limit. In recent years, however, the spring chinook population has been on the

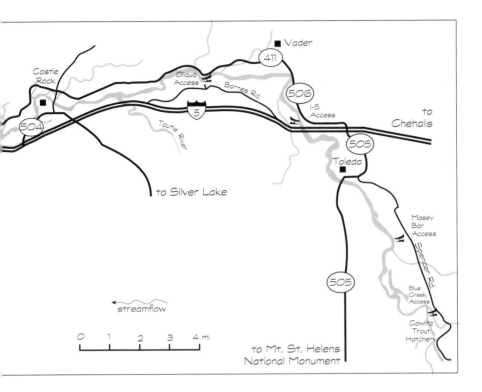

decline throughout the Northwest. Conservation is the key to assuring that they remain among our spring fishing opportunities.

Spring chinook can be taken by a variety of methods. We trolled herring, but trolled spinners also work well, as does backbouncing plugs, clusters of salmon roe, or sand shrimp. When backbouncing or trolling, keep your offering on the bottom, because that's where the chinook hang out.

There are many places along the Cowlitz where bank anglers can get a shot at these fish. Driving down Highway 411 between Vader and Longview, I have seen several areas where anglers (mostly plunkers) have gained access to the river and fished for springers. Farther upstream, just below the salmon hatchery's barrier dam, is another popular spot for anglers seeking spring chinook. Salmon

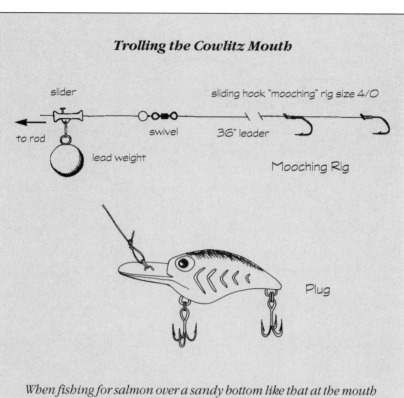

Trolling the Cowlitz Mouth

slider

sliding hook "mooching" rig size 4/O

to rod

swivel   36" leader

lead weight

Mooching Rig

Plug

When fishing for salmon over a sandy bottom like that at the mouth of the Cowlitz, herring and a standard salmon mooching rig is most often used. Troll slowly, making sure the weight is just heavy enough to keep the herring near the bottom. Trolling plugs is also effective in this type of water.

When fishing drifts upstream, either from shore or out of a boat, use basic steelhead-style tackle (spinner or bait). Find a likely drift and, again, using just enough weight to keep the offering near the bottom, bounce the bait through.

roe clusters and sand shrimp bounced along the bottom are the usual baits up here.

April and May are good months to try for springers in the Cowlitz, but run size, river conditions, and regulations vary considerably from year to year. Be sure to check the current regulations. Blue Creek Bait and Tackle (360-864-6015) usually has up-to-the-minute information about the Cowlitz in the vicinity of the hatchery. Barrier Dam Campground (360-985-2495) is a good source of information about the river between the barrier dam (six miles upriver) and Blue Creek.

The floods of 1996 and 1997 wrecked havoc with boat ramps on the lower Cowlitz. At this time, best boat access is at Longview (Gerhart Gardens, a Longview municipal facility at the west end of the Highway 432 bridge), at a Weyerhaueser ramp on the Columbia north of the Cowlitz mouth, and at the mouth of the Kalama in the town of Kalama. Further upstream, boaters can put in at Olequa (just north of Castle Rock about four miles above the mouth of the Toutle on the east bank of the Cowlitz), and at Blue Creek Ramp near the trout hatchery.

A number of other Washington rivers offer good springer fishing. In the same vicinity as the Cowlitz, the mouth of the Kalama is a popular spot. Boat anglers launch at the I-5 Bridge and a mile or so upstream.

Also close by and hosting spring chinook, is the Lewis River (North Fork). The most popular stretch on the Lewis is near the Cedar Creek Boat Ramp, but there is plenty of other good water in both directions. Lewis River Sports in Woodland (360-225-9530) is a good source for information on this fishery.

Bottomfishing

Neah Bay, mid-April

Showers turned to downpour as we reached Clallam Bay. Our destination was Neah Bay, just four miles from Cape Flattery, the westernmost point in the contiguous United States.

The community of Neah Bay is within the boundaries of the Makah Indian Reservation and is the gateway to some of the best saltwater fishing off the Washington coast. To reach it, follow State Highway 112 west from Port Angeles, or Highway 101 north to its junction with Highway 112 at Clallum Bay.

Neah Bay is carved out of a majestic landscape of towering cliffs, rock walls, and pinnacles. Blemished only by distant logging clearcuts, it is one of the last remaining truly wild areas of Washington state, and its beauty alone is worth a visit.

Pinky Freeman and I make an annual trip to Neah Bay just after the lingcod opener. The weather here is always a gamble, but rain seldom dampens our spirits or shuts us down. The wind can be another story. If it's too windy, we can't get Pinky's 17-foot Boston Whaler out of the boat basin.

We weighed our options as we settled into our motel room. Then we took care of our boat moorage and launch fee with Big Salmon Fishing Resort and headed out to Waadah Island. Waadah is just outside the boat basin and is connected to land by the jetty that protects the bay. From past trips, we knew Waadah would be a good choice if the wind prevented us from cruising to our favorite fishing grounds farther west.

We might also have headed for Seal and Sail Rocks, two towering monoliths a 15-minute run east from the boat basin. They mark a fairly shallow area and offer shelter as well as good catches of

Black rockfish are most abundant in the catch around Neah Bay.

rockfish and lingcod. If the weather is suitable for fishing around Waadah Island, it's usually OK to make the run down to Seal and Sail.

The water around Waadah was choppy enough that we decided to remain there for the afternoon. We would head west later that evening if things died down. Pinky and I prefer to use fly gear to fish for black rockfish, but that was out of the question in this wind. So we opted for light spinning tackle, which is almost as fun.

There are several species of bottomfish that can be taken in the relatively shallow waters around Neah Bay. The most frequent catches on light tackle are black rockfish, greenling, lingcod, and (in lesser numbers) a variety of other types of rockfish. Black rockfish, often mistakenly called sea bass, are the most abundant.

As their name implies, rockfish can be found along the rocky coastline or over a rocky bottom. Ranging in size from one to six pounds (in most areas), they are aggressive predators and will take

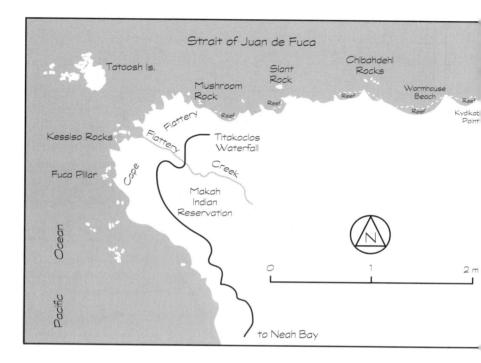

Strait of Juan de Fuca

Tatoosh Is.

Mushroom
Rock

Slant
Rock

Chibahdehl
Rocks

Warmhouse
Beach

Reef

Reef

Reef

Reef

Flattery

Reef

Kydikab
Point

Kessiso Rocks

Flattery

Titakoclos
Waterfall

Flattery

Creek

Fuca Pillar

Cape

Makah
Indian
Reservation

N

Ocean

0   1   2 m

Pacific

to Neah Bay

nearly anything they can fit into their mouths. When taken in shallow water, they fight very much like a largemouth bass of similar
size.

The Neah Bay area is perfect rockfish habitat, offering both a
rocky shoreline and a rocky bottom. Since these are schooling fish,
where you catch one, you will usually find plenty more. The key is
to put your offering on the bottom and retrieve or jig it in an erratic
manner. When you get into a school of blacks, the action can be fast
and furious.

Pinky and I had decided to fish the east side of Waadah Island,
which is sheltered from the wind and from the heavy swells that
were rolling in from the west with increasing ferocity. The water
was 20- or 30-feet deep. We knotted half-ounce leadhead jigs to our
lines and attached plastic, curlytailed grubs to the hooks. Pinky slid
on a white grub, and I chose a brown one, both proven colors.

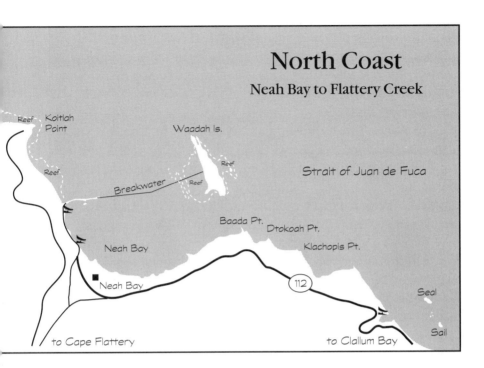

North Coast
Neah Bay to Flattery Creek

Reef Koitlah Point

Waadah Is.

Reef

Reef

Breakwater Reef

Strait of Juan de Fuca

Baada Pt.

Dtokoah Pt.

Neah Bay

Klachopis Pt.

Neah Bay

112

Seal

to Cape Flattery

to Clallum Bay

Sail

We picked up a couple of small blacks in and around the floating kelp 30 or 40 feet off shore, then eased our way around the island to a point of rocks that protrudes out into the water. We cast towards shore and reeled in quickly to avoid the tackle-hungry bottom. On nearly every cast, we hooked a fish and quickly reached our limit of 10 rockfish each.

That night the brunt of the storm hit, and the next morning we couldn't even get our boat out of the boat basin, so we headed home.

On another spring visit to Neah Bay with friends Terry Sheely and Joe George, the weather was quite a different story. Our arrival found the skies clear and the water flat as a pancake. Since we never know how long good weather will last on the north coast at this time of the year, we headed directly for Tatoosh Island, where the Cape Flattery Lighthouse rises from among the rocks.

It takes calm seas to get all the way to Tatoosh, then around the "corner" to the Flattery Creek area, which my buddies have nicknamed *The Promised Land*. This is the very best area I have found for really big rockfish and lingcod, and when weather permits, it is always our first choice.

To get to The Promised Land, you must first pass between Tatoosh Island and the mainland, an area of exposed rock that can eat a small boat. On this trip we were in Terry's 16-foot Lund with 70-horse outboard, a capable craft if the weather is calm and the operator has experience in the open ocean. A sharp eye and a fine-tuned motor are essential for running the gamut of rock pinnacles that pierce the water throughout this area.

Safest passage can be made during the incoming tide, which also offers the best fishing, especially when the difference between low and high tides is not extreme. The absolute best fishing is often in the last two hours before high tide, and in the slack water immediately following. However, there are exceptions, and fish can usually be taken during all tidal phases.

On this day, the water around the corner was calmer than I had ever seen it. Conditions were ideal for fly fishing. To fly fish for rockfish and lings, you usually need a heavy sinking, or sinking-tip line. A Teeny 400-grain sinking-tip line is my preference. This line will let me fish down to about 40 feet if there isn't too much current. Leaders need not be over three feet in length, and 25-pound-test hard mono will withstand the abrasion of barnacled rocks, at least for awhile.

Fly patterns don't need to be fancy. Over the years, I have found that simple, durable patterns, such as flies tied completely of dyed rabbitstrip, are highly effective. Most of the time I use a fly that I call "Halfarabbit." I tie it in a host of colors and in sizes 2 through 6/0. For black rockfish, an orange, red, or white Halfarabbit in size 1/0 is my usual choice. General baitfish patterns that resemble herring, anchovies, or candlefish also work well.

Due to the weight of the heavy shooting heads, large flies, and

relentless wind, rods for line weights 8 through 10 are most practical. I generally fish with a 10-weight outfit in case I get into a big lingcod.

Sometimes rockfish can even be taken on a floating line. You might see them feeding on baitfish, especially during low-light hours near shore. The baitfish will actually break the surface, with rockfish right on their tail. At other times during the spring, black rockfish will fin the surface as they feed on megalops, which are the last stage of the crab larvae before they settle to the ocean floor. In either case, I switch to a floating line and large saltwater poppers.

Although less likely to be taken by light tackle anglers, lingcod are often available in rockfish water. Their sparser presence in the day's catch is due to their smaller population, and to the fact that rockfish usually grab your offering first!

The fight of a large lingcod is brutal. Incredibly strong and aggressive foragers, they will pursue fish nearly as large as themselves. Many times lingcod are caught when they attack smaller fish that are already on the line. The ling has a hard time releasing the smaller fish if you keep constant pressure on it.

Lingcod can grow to five feet in length. When a large one is hooked, it can put up quite a tussle. The key is to get it off the bottom as quickly as possible to prevent it from sticking its head into a hole in the rocks, after which you will never get it up. My usual tackle for lingcod in the Flattery Creek area is pipe jigs, jigheads with scampi, or big curlytailed jigs in the two- to six-ounce range. Some anglers swear by bait (herring is most popular), and it certainly works, but I have never felt there was a significant advantage to its use.

You can catch lingcod along rocky shorelines, but the best chance for a huge ling is in deeper, more isolated water. The Flattery Creek area is ideal.

On that exceptionally calm day in The Promised Land with Terry and Joe, we were fishing close to a pinnacle, closer than I had ever been. I had switched from my fly rod to a halibut rod—a short, stout stick with a levelwind reel loaded with 80-pound test braided dacron line. The drag on the reel was clamped down so tight that I couldn't even pull line off with my hands. A six-ounce leadhead and scampi was attached to a shock tippet of 60-pound test braided wire. I was all set for the big guy—I thought.

Terry moved the boat in as close as he dared. I dropped the big scampi to the bottom and, in just a few jigs of the rod, I had a solid hookup. Having fished for big halibut in Alaska, I knew this fish was significant. Gaining line as fast as I could, I pumped and reeled, pumped and reeled, putting 30, maybe 40 feet of line back on my spool. Then, in three quick runs, the fish was back on the bottom. The next few seconds consisted of an intense tug-o-war in which I was the loser. Shaking, I reeled up my jigless line, and we all sat there for a long moment in utter silence. We didn't even bother fishing any more. One hookup with a nuclear sub per day is my limit.

Ocean Charters, early May

I hovered close to the coffee machine, trying desperately to achieve consciousness. My system just didn't like the idea of getting up at 4 a.m., but as on many another fishing morning, I knew I would survive. The charter office of Big Salmon  Fishing Resort in Neah Bay, was beginning to fill up with customers for the day's halibut excursion. A final head tally confirmed that all parties were present, and we began our gear-toting trek to the fog-choked boat basin where the *Blue Chip* was waiting.

The big diesels growled as they spewed out their sickening, eye-burning fumes. After another head count, our skipper skillfully backed the 43-foot sportfishing vessel out of its stall, and we began our hour-long cruise to the halibut grounds of Swiftsure Bank.

As we neared our destination, giant swells rocked the boat like a toy in a tub. By the time we reached the fishing grounds, a few of the queasy sorts began their day-long ordeal of hanging their heads over the boat's railing before returning to the cabin in varying shades of green. The hardy among us waited patiently for the command from the skipper to drop our jigs. When the word came, the heavy pipe and scampi jigs slid 360 feet down to the bottom.

Halibut most often hang out on the bottom. The secret to successful halibut fishing is getting your jig to the bottom quickly, then keeping up a steady two-foot jigging action. Sounds easy, but working a 32-oz. jig tied to 80-lb. test braided dacron in 360 feet of water is hard work!

Best halibut fishing off the Washington coast is at Swiftsure Bank.

I was lucky. No sooner did my jig hit the bottom, then I felt it come into solid contact with something. Since we were fishing over a sandy bottom, I pretty much knew what the subsequent heave of my rod would prove. I hit it with all my might, and the battle was on. It seemed as though I would gain 10 feet of line, and then the fish would take 20. Ten minutes into the battle, my nerves as well as my muscles were wearing thin. When the deckhand brought me the fighting belt (a leather belt with a cup in front for the rodbutt), it became much easier, but the battle was far from over.

The giant flatfish tore around in a series of wild runs and tackle-testing maneuvers near the surface. The deckhand was by my side, ready with the harpoon as the halibut came into view, a violent charge to the surface that tangled my line with others. The skipper was desperately trying to cut it free when the halibut made a wild splash on the surface, and it was all over. The jig broke free, and we stared, winded and unbelieving, as the halibut began its graceful wave-like glide back to the bottom.

We took several other halibut that day, the largest weighing in around 50 pounds. Although not as plentiful or large as halibut from grounds farther north, good catches are often made close to home. Most are well under 50 pounds, but the state record is a whopping 288 pounds.

The best halibut fishing off the Washington coast is at Swiftsure Bank and a few other locations inside the Strait of Juan de Fuca. Several charters in the Neah Bay area target halibut during the open season, which currently begins May 1 for waters west of Tatoosh, and May 23 for waters to the east. The season remains open until the quota is taken. For information, call the WDFW Sport Fishing Hotline (206-976-3200) or Big Salmon Resort (360-645-2374). Big Salmon operates a fleet of charter boats out of Neah Bay. In the Sekiu/Clallam Bay area, call the Clallum Bay-Sekiu Chamber of Commerce (360-963-2339) for a list of charter operators.

The halibut catch is significantly less in Washington's southern waters, but other bottomfish species are taken in great numbers out of Westport (on Grays Harbor) and Ilwaco (near the mouth of the Columbia). For a complete list of charters out of Westport, contact the Westport Chamber of Commerce (360-268-9422), and for Ilwaco, the Long Beach Chamber (360-642-2400).

Shad

Columbia River, May

I was skeptical at first. I didn't know what shad fishing could do for me. I had begun to think of myself as a trout fisherman, a diehard chaser of rainbows, browns, and cutthroat. But because I couldn't come up with a good enough excuse, I found myself headed for Bonneville Dam in the company of a couple other (more enthusiastic) shad first-timers.

We had gotten a report that shad were thick below the dam and that anglers were yanking these giant herring-like fish out of the water right and left. It sounded at the very least—interesting.

When we pulled into the parking area below the dam, there were only four or five parked cars. We couldn't help wondering, *Why so few cars if the fishing's hot?* After tackling a fisherman and inquiring about the action, we found out. So far this morning, only two or three shad had been landed. Most anglers had already given up in disgust. When the fisherman broke my hold, he too tromped off towards his car.

More skeptical than ever, I started out using a light fly rod and a tiny size 10 white bucktail streamer. We had been told that shad would hit almost anything white, as long as it's small. Shad prefer small food items because they have little mouths. To catch these fish on a fly, according to our sources, you simply make short casts with a sinking line, strip your fly back in with short quick jerks, and the shad will stack up on the bank behind you like cordwood.

An hour later I was still wondering what shad fishing could do for me. I sat down on a rock to ponder over a brew, when a spin-fishing gent upstream tied into a fish. WOW! I watched in amazement as the fish tore off, obviously exerting tremendous energy in

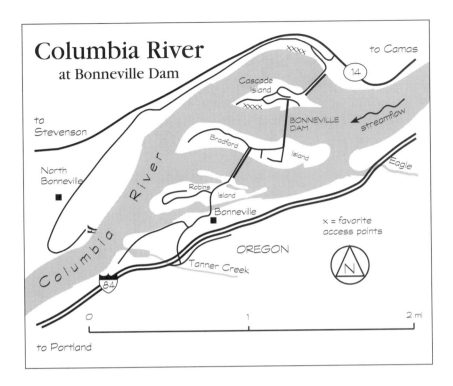

Columbia River
at Bonneville Dam

to Camas

to Stevenson

Cascade Island

BONNEVILLE DAM

streamflow

Bradford

Island

Eagle

North Bonneville

Robins Island

Bonneville

x = favorite access points

OREGON

Tanner Creek

Columbia River

84

to Portland

0   1   2 mi

an effort to shake that nasty hook. It looked for all the world like a steelhead battle, and as I moved closer for a better view, I guessed the fish's weight at about four pounds. When the shad was netted, I couldn't believe how bright it was. I stared at it for a long time, having never seen one before. Then suddenly it clicked; I knew what shad fishing could do for me. I raced back to my spot below the dam.

Obviously, fishing wasn't super hot that day, but seeing that one shad gave me a whole new outlook. I switched from fly rod to a medium-weight spinning rod in order to reach moving water, which the successful angler upstream said was a necessity. I knotted on a one-sixteenth ounce white, curlytailed crappie jig, which (you guessed it) is what he was using.

After only a few casts, using the same tackle, my partner hooked a fish that put up a nearly identical battle. Shad are truly remarkable fighters—quick, powerful, and aggressive to the very end.

White (or American) shad are one of the most plentiful species in the Columbia River system, yet there is probably no fish more overlooked by Washington state anglers.

Shad return to the Columbia on their spawning run in May and June, ascending the ladders at Bonneville Dam by the hundreds of thousands. Biologists believe water temperature plays a key role in shad migrations. Temperatures in the low to mid-sixties stimulate peak movement upriver.

The white shad is flat (from side to side) with a narrow bluish green back, large silver side scales, and a deeply forked tail. Weights average three to five pounds, with males smaller than females. Shad reach sexual maturity at three to five years. Spawners pair up over sand or gravel, where the female deposits a few hundred thousand eggs to be fertilized by her companion. The eggs are carried in the current before they absorb water and sink. Eggs hatch in about eight days, and the half-inch fry remain in fresh water until late fall, when survivors head for the sea. They remain in salt water until fully mature and ready to spawn.

I returned to Bonneville Dam a few days later. This time the parking lot on Cascades Island was packed, and at least a hundred anglers lined the bank. Many of them had bent rods.

An angler in the know explained to me that poor fishing on my previous trip was due to the fact that the floodgates closest to shore had been closed. Shad seek out fast current, and if the near gates are closed, there's less good current within casting range.

This time the gates were open, and a strong current passed close to the island. Catching the current just right is always a gamble. Dam spills on the Columbia are controlled by computers. Factors such as water flow, rainfall, and irrigation all affect the system. But even if the water is off when you arrive, you can get into fish with a little extra work, and the near gates are seldom down for extended periods. If they're closed one day, more than likely they'll be open the next.

We eventually found a spot along the bank. On our previous trip, we had to cast far out into the mainstream, with additional

Shad return to the Columbia on their spawning run in May or June.

weight clamped to our lines to fight the wind that seems to blow incessantly upriver. This time, only a short cast was needed to find the fish.

We released most of our catch, but I kept several (there's no limit in Washington). I had tasted canned smoked shad before (delicious!) and was looking forward to more. Canning softens the bones, which are plentiful and problematic for the chef and several of the eaters at my house.

Columbia shad migrations are monitored at the fish ladders located at each dam along the river. Daily tallies of fish going through the ladders appear in local newspapers, and this is the best way to determine when to hit the river. When the daily count reaches 20,000 fish at the Bonneville ladder, the peak is near. Peak migration can last several weeks, with tallies of 20,000 to 75,000 fish daily.

Most shad fishing on the Columbia is in the tailraces below the lowest few dams. I have only fished for them on Cascade Island, which connects to Bonneville Dam on the downstream side. The long rocky shoreline on the south side of the island attracts most of the anglers, but at times you can find fish on the other side of the island if the appropriate flood gates are open. People seem to bunch up near the deadline 600 feet below the dam, and it does seem that the closer to the deadline, the better the fishing.

Boaters do well at the mouth of the Washougal River between the towns of Camas and Washougal, and at many other places on the river where the current is fast, though the stretch below Bonneville Dam is certainly the hot spot. Anglers also find shad plentiful below the next couple of dams upstream.

Spinning rigs and small jigs are the most popular gear for shad fishing. White and silver crappie jigs in sizes one-sixteenth to one-eighth ounce seem to produce best. Be sure to keep your offering small. I have even done well with jigheads alone, without the curly tail, when the fish were in thick.

Light- to medium-weight spinning outfits are the most practical for shad fishing. Six-to 10-pound test monofilament line is adequate. I usually go with the heavier line simply because of the inevitable rock abrasion fishing close to shore.

Although not as easy (simply because of the topography), you can fly fish for shad below the dam if conditions are right. I limit my fly casting to those times when there are few people on the island and the wind is not howling up the river—which is seldom. It's just too dangerous flinging a fly line around when there is a lot of foot traffic moving up and down the shore. Fly fishing from a boat is another matter, and I have friends who do it successfully in the lower river.

To fly fish from shore, you'll need a 7- to 9-weight system in order to cast the heavy, sinking shooting head that will get you down to fish in the fast currents. I prefer a Teeny 200 grain line on a 7-weight, fast action graphite rod. However, a variety of shooting heads is advisable due to the changing water flows. If you can't get to the shad, you can't catch them!

Fly leaders don't seem to be a factor. The shad certainly aren't leader shy, and your leaders don't have to be tapered or of fine diameter. A short, level section of leader will work quite nicely. Due to the abrasive rocks, you should check your leader for nicks often.

Since shad don't feed once they enter fresh water, why they hit artificial flies remains nebulous. Maybe they hit them out of aggravation, or just from force of habit. For whatever reason, Columbia shad really slam any small streamer or bucktail that passes in front of them. I have had my best action with a simple pattern tied on a size 10 streamer hook, with a body of silver mylar and a tiny wing of white calftail. Most shad flies I've seen are of similar design. But style is less important than size. Small flies (sizes 10 or 8) out-produce larger ones.

There are no real tricks to fly casting for shad. Cast upstream, and let your line sink and swing with the current. When the shad are in thick, there is often a strike on nearly every cast. Just remember to cast into the current, and use enough weight so that your fly sinks down to the shad's level. There is no question as to the take. Shad hit hard, but remember, their mouths are soft. Care must be taken during the battle, and you should expect many LDRs (long distance releases).

Many anglers who fish below the dams leave with gunny sacks stuffed full of shad, as their flesh and roe are superb when properly prepared. Although the supply of shad seems endless right now, I'm sure that steelhead, salmon, and trout were once as plentiful. It isn't too early to begin thinking in terms of moderation and conservation where this great game fish is concerned.

Surf and Jetty Fishing

Half-Moon Bay, early June

I followed the receding water out as far as I dared, cast with a giant heave, then ran back up the beach as fast as I could to beat the incoming waves. It was important to keep all the slack out of the line, because detecting a strike in the pounding surf took total concentration.

I was fishing beside the westernmost finger jetty of Westport's Half-Moon Bay. The finger jetties are a series of short rock outcroppings built to protect the dock area of this coastal fishing community in southwest Washington. In spring, redtail surfperch can be caught right in the surf here. I like fishing this little bay because it is sheltered by the big jetty that protects Westport, and its tidal action is much calmer than that of the Pacific beaches nearby.

I was using a medium weight spinning outfit and reel loaded with 10-pound test line and baited with sandshrimp (ghost shrimp). A sliding, one-ounce pyramid sinker was attached above the swivel that connected the foot-long leader. My method was straightforward. I cast out and waited for the slightest movement of the line. I set the hook at the tiniest twitch, keeping constant pressure on the fish. On this day, more often than not, a perch would hit only moments after the big sinker touched down.

Since surfperch are schooling fish, it is often easy to hook many perch on an outing (though the limit is one per person). The hardest part is finding them to begin with.

The best way to locate good redtail surfperch water is to identify likely holding areas at low tide, then return when the tide is coming in. Look for depressions or pockets in the sand, or for rocky areas where perch might feed on the incoming tide. Sometimes I

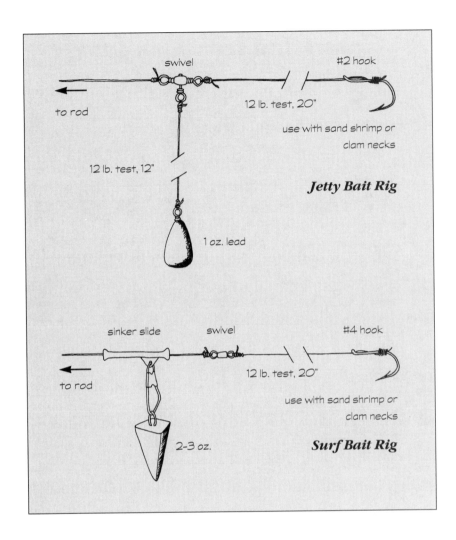

Jetty Bait Rig

swivel

#2 hook

to rod

12 lb. test, 20"

use with sand shrimp or clam necks

12 lb. test, 12"

1 oz. lead

sinker slide

swivel

#4 hook

to rod

12 lb. test, 20"

use with sand shrimp or clam necks

2-3 oz.

Surf Bait Rig

place a little pile of rocks directly up the beach from a likely spot so that I can find it when the tide is high. I have always done best for surfperch from about an hour before high tide until an hour or so after the change.

Although I usually choose to fish at Half Moon Bay, many anglers prefer casting into the open ocean. You can use the same technique, but you'll need a longer and stiffer rod, with about two ounces of lead to contend with the heavier wave action.

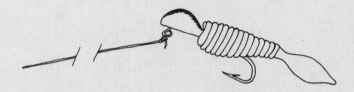

Leadhead Jig

For an even simpler rig, good for jetty or surf, try leadheads with plastic curlytailed grubs. For rockfish, I use a quarter- ounce leadhead on a medium weight rod loaded with 10-pound test line. For lingcod, I move up to a one-ounce leadhead, a heavy spinning rod, and a reel loaded with 25-pound test line.

Sometimes you can get into surfperch while fishing off the finger jetties, but I have found this to be spotty, at best.

The jetties are good producers for a variety of other bottom species though, and I fish several of them often. Besides the finger jetties in Westport, the large guarding jetties of Westport, Fort Canby (at the Mouth of the Columbia), and Ocean Shores (across Grays Harbor from Westport) get a lot of my attention.

Be advised that jetty fishing requires some agility, as there's a lot of boulder hopping involved, and they can be dangerous for those who are not sure-footed.

Along the jetties you will find rockfish, lingcod, greenling, flounder, and the occasional perch as well as a few other bottom species. Since most of these fish are schooling by nature, you will usually have to move around a bit to find them. Sometimes this is easy—and sometimes it takes all day.

Weather permitting, the best way to fish the jetties is from a small boat. I have fished from boats as small as 14-footers along the harbor side of jetties at Westport and Fort Canby. This should only be done on the calmest of days, and it's imperative to pay close attention to tide and weather conditions. Obviously, it is much easier

The best time to fish for surfperch is about an hour before high tide until an hour or so after the change.

to locate fish while cruising along the jetty in a boat than while stumbling among the rocks. It also saves wear and tear on your line. Sometimes catches along the jetties can be as good as at the rockpiles farther out, which are usually only accessible to commercial charters.

Summer

It seemed just yesterday that trout were rising enthusiastically to midge imitations fished on the surface. Today, it just wasn't going to happen. I checked the water temperature, and the 70 degree reading confirmed—it was too warm for these rainbows to make a daytime appearance. The recent bout of 95-degree weather had put a check on this little lake until the fall cool-down. There would still be trout in my fishing picture, but not here. It was time to move on, but to what? and where? As usual, there were many possibilities.

The perennial Washington angler's lament—so many fish, so little time—reaches its peak intensity in summer. Summer steelhead are in the coastal rivers, many bass and trout lakes are in their prime, inland streams are thick with insect hatches and eager trout, salmon and bottomfish are still available at the coast, little creeks and ponds are open throughout the state, and the mountain lakes beckon with their offer of hungry trout in an alpine setting.

If you're like me, you want to do it all—an impossible challenge. Still, one does one's best.

Summer Steelhead

Kalama River, early July

When Mark Miller, my steelheading buddy, turned his truck off I-5 onto the Kalama River Road, an orange tint was just beginning to light the eastern sky above dark, tree-covered hills. As we stepped out of the truck, we knew it was  going to be a warm day. We didn't even need long-sleeved shirts. It would be the kind of summer day most westsiders look forward to. But not steelheaders. We would only have two, maybe three hours tops before the sun spoiled our fishing.

Every summer, Mark and I try to squeeze in a trip or two to this southwest Washington river. This year, the Kalama was rumored to be full of fish. Mark rigged up with sandshrimp, one of the most popular and productive baits for summer steelhead.

Spinner and spoon anglers also do very well on this river. Since it is a relatively small river, covering the water while fishing around structure like boulders and along banks is a breeze with appropriate spinning tackle. Small spinners and spoons are the rule in the Kalama's clear summer flows, with many steelhead taken on trout-size spinners (size range 2-3).

I opted for my usual fly tackle, also productive, though in sheer numbers of fish hooked, nowhere near as effective as bait.

To fly fish the Kalama at summer flow, I use a floating line on a 7-weight rod and a handful of low-water summer steelhead flies such as Skunk, Skykomish, Sunrise, Burlap, Fall Favorite, Orange Heron, or Teeny Nymph. I don't think pattern matters much. To narrow my choices, if for no other reason, I usually go with the dark day/dark fly, bright day/bright fly theory, which seems to work as well as anything.

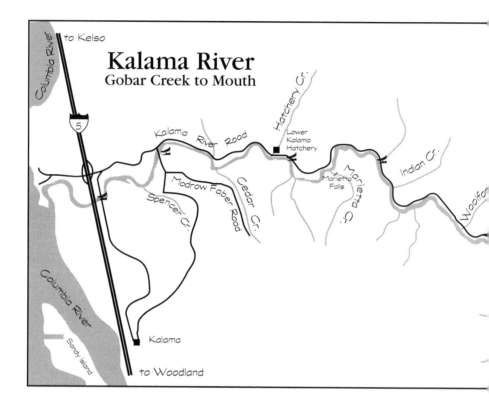

Kalama River
Gobar Creek to Mouth

The area we were fishing was broken by protruding boulders and riffles, perfect for steelhead at this time of year. When water temperature rises in summer, steelhead seek out this kind of water for its higher oxygen content. We directed our casts to the whitewater near boulders and to the deeper sections of the riffles.

Mark was the first to yell "fish on," which came as no surprise since he is one of the best steelheaders I know. A few minutes later, he was kneeling in the gravel, gently working water through the gills of a seven-pound hen. When she regained her strength, she shot from his hands and disappeared into the river.

Working our way upstream, Mark and I each hooked and lost a fish. Soon, the sun was beating down on the water, sending the fish for cover and diminishing our odds for a hook-up. After an hour of lackadaisical casting, we called it quits.

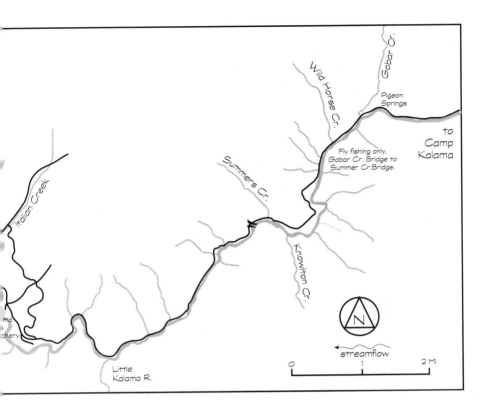

Once the sun chases me off the Kalama, I always take a slow drive along the river road to see if I can spot fish. I stop at each wide spot in the road and scrutinize the river through polarized lenses. If I see fish, I'm always tempted to give them a cast or two. I have yielded to that temptation countless times, but my efforts almost always end in disappointment. When the sun is on the water, the Kalama's steelhead get lockjaw.

Cloudy days are quite a different story. Then, spotting fish from the road is often the first step toward a catch. I will often walk along the road, and when I see a fish, I mentally mark its location with an object on the river or on shore—a rock, bush, or tree. After scrambling down to the river well upstream of the marked location, I delicately work a fly down toward the marked fish, then pound that area for all it's worth. This tactic often pays off. The secret is to find fish that have not yet been spooked by a careless angler.

In recent years, access to the Kalama has become a problem. Long stretches of the river run through private property, and a lot of it is posted. There are still a reasonable number of access points, though, and they are obvious as you drive the river road. A pullover and a trail leading to the water is a good indication that it's okay to fish in that spot. There are also bank fishing opportunities at the five boat ramps on the 20-mile stretch of the river open to steelheading.

To reach the river, take the Kalama River Road exit off I-5, just north of the town of Kalama. There is excellent water for driftboat and bank angling throughout the stretch from Modrow Bridge all the way up to the posted boundary at Gobar Creek Bridge, approximately 17 miles. The lowest drift on the river is from Modrow Bridge (on Kalama River Rd.) to the Interstate bridge. Power boats are not allowed above Modrow, and most hang out below the Interstate bridge, fishing the slack water just before its confluence with the Columbia.

The Kalama also has a fly fishing-only section between Summer Creek Bridge and Gobar Creek Bridge at the upper boundary of the open water, roughly three miles. This is a very good piece of water, but no better, in my opinion, than others downstream. From September 1 through October 31, the lower river from the hatchery pump intakes to the gas pipeline crossing at Mahaffey Campground is also limited to fly fishing-only.

One of the best sources for information about the river is Prichard's Western Angler (360-673-4690) on Kalama River Road. A lot of anglers stop by here, and a wealth of information is left at the doorstep.

Hoh River, late July

erb Jacobsen rowed his new driftboat ashore at the head of the first drift, and we both piled out, anxious to wet a line. From the way we were acting, you would think neither of us got much chance to fish. In reality, Herb is a fishing guide on several of the Olympic Peninsula's steelhead rivers, and I was nearing completion of a book on the Hoh River and had been steelheading there on a regular basis for the past year. I can only say, with no apologies, that steelheading has that effect on me. It seems I can never get enough!

Herb and I had fished this hole together several times during the past year. One of our favorites, it's located on the Upper Hoh near the last boat ramp just inside the Olympic National Park boundary. The Upper Hoh is generally considered to be that portion of the river above the Highway 101 bridge.

This drift was typical of the upper river. The rocky bar we were standing on tapered to a moderately flowing run, broken in places by larger boulders, a few of which projected above the river's surface. Its deepest section—six to eight feet— stretched along the alder-lined bank on the far side of the river.

Wading a glacial stream like the Hoh is a bit tricky. Underwater visibility is never better than two feet due to the constant flow of glacial scour. By experience, I have learned that a dunk in the Hoh is to be avoided at all cost (think of the river as freshly melted ice).

Herb began working the head of the run while I cast to the tailout; both of us were using fly rods. Within minutes, Herb hooked a fish. I scrambled up to his position, camera in hand, to record the action for my new book. It was a small steelhead, but beautiful just the same. It was our only fish of the day.

Steelhead fishing is never a sure thing. Steelhead fly fishing is even less predictable. And steelhead fly fishing on big glacial rivers like

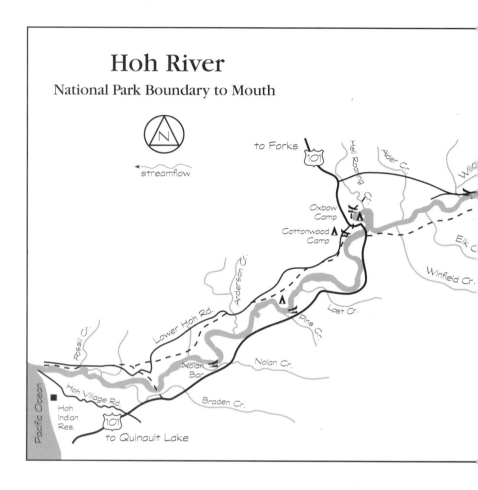

Hoh River

National Park Boundary to Mouth

streamflow

to Forks
101

Hell Roaring Cr.

Alder Cr.

Wild

Oxbow
Camp

Cottonwood
Camp

Elk C

Winfield Cr.

Anderson Cr.

Lost Cr.

Pins Cr.

Lower Hoh Rd.

Fossil Cr.

Nolan Cr.

Nolan
Bar

Hoh Village Rd.

Braden Cr.

Pacific Ocean

Hoh
Indian
Res.

101

to Quinault Lake

the Hoh is always a gamble.

When fishing here, I use the same techniques as on smaller, clearer streams, except that I usually choose a large, brightly colored fly. I figure the fish can't see any better through the cloudy water than I can.

Conventional steelhead tackle is much more productive here than fly gear. Most Hoh steelheaders use a large spinning or casting rod with 10- to 14-pound monofilament, and bait, spoons, plugs, or spinners.

The Hoh flow is relatively stable in summer. Summer rains don't have the "oomph" of the winter storms, which can send the

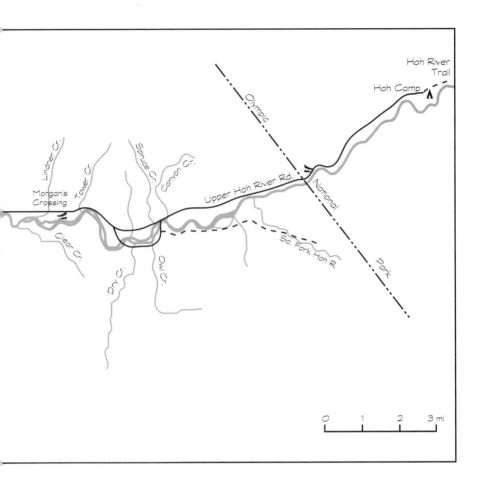

river into flood stage overnight. In fact, summer rains often exert a positive influence, bringing new fish into the river and revitalizing those already here.

Driftboats are popular on the Hoh, especially on the lower river where bank fishing opportunities are less plentiful; I have seen as many as 15 driftboats slide by in July. The highest public ramp is just inside the National Park boundary. Moving downstream, there are improved ramps at Morgan's Crossing Camp, The Oxbow Camp, Cottonwood Camp, and Nolan Bar. There are also several spots along the Upper Hoh Road where the river comes in contact with the highway and boats can be safely launched. The Oxbow ramp (at the Highway 101 bridge) and Cottonwood ramp (on Oil City Road) are generally used for launching, while Nolan Bar (also off Highway 101) is used as a take-out.

Though floating is the most popular way to fish the Hoh, it's a great river to explore on foot. The Upper Hoh River Road offers easy access to the north bank above Willoughby Creek. Two of my favorite summer steelhead bank fisheries are at Morgan's Crossing on the upper river, and near Nolan Bar on the lower stretch. At the end of the road, the Hoh River Trail follows the stream towards its source on Mt. Olympus, though the river is closed to steelhead angling above the park boundary. Like many streams hosting anadramous runs, the Hoh is tightly regulated.

For an update on fishing conditions for the Hoh and other Olympic Peninsula streams, or to arrange for a guide, contact Olympic Sporting Goods in Forks at (360-374-6330). Other good summer steelhead streams in the Hoh River-Forks area include the Quillayute, Sol Duc, and Calawah rivers. Further north are the Elwah and Lyre rivers.

Lodging and guide services are available at the Westward Hoh Resort (360-374-6657). The Hoh River Resort (360-374-5566) offers RV hookups, groceries, and tackle. Most other amenities of civilization can be found in the town of Forks. There are four campgrounds on the lower Hoh and along nearby rivers. The largest campground in the area is at Bogachiel State Park, about five miles south of Forks on Highway 101.

Cowlitz River, early August

I've got a big one! I've got a big one!" my wife shouted.

I was downstream a ways, and it took me awhile to get up to where Cindy was fishing.

"What should I do? Aaah! What should I do?"

She was in a genuine panic. And rightly so. We were fishing for cutthroat when her size 0 Mepps spinner was intercepted by a summer steelhead.

When I saw the seriousness of the situation, I loosened her drag and advised, "Don't do anything; just keep the slack out of your line."

I was reasonably sure she would loose the fish. This was her first steelhead hook-up, and she was using an ultralight rod with four-pound monofilament. I couldn't feel confident about the outcome.

But the fish gods were on her side. Cindy played and landed the six-pound summer steelhead. Beginner's luck!

That incident took place many years ago on the Cowlitz River, a tributary of the Columbia which consistently gives up more steelhead to anglers than any other river in the state. The estimated catch figure for summer fish alone during 1993 was 8,082 fish according to WDFW. Twice that number are usually recorded during the winter season!

The first time I boated the Cowlitz with friends, I wasn't at all prepared for the encounter. It was early morning when we arrived at the launch below the trout hatchery off Spencer Road west of the town of Cowlitz. Though barely light, there was already a line of jet sleds waiting to launch. And other boats quickly lined up behind us.

The lower river was thick with boats, a circus without a ringmaster! Most boaters drifted with the current, tossing bait. After making a pass through what they thought was the good water, they would run back to their starting point and begin again. Meanwhile, other boats were back-trolling lures through the same water. Still others anchored in the midst of this mayhem. If it wasn't for the fact that everyone seemed to be catching fish, we would have left without regrets.

Instead, we moved downstream to where the crowd thinned out a bit and began fishing. Even here, there were more boats on the water than I had ever seen, except perhaps at buoy 10 on the Columbia.

The Cowlitz is generally regarded as "a boater's river," but there are also places where the Cowlitz is easily fished from shore. The most popular steelhead bank fishery on the river is just downstream from the trout hatchery, at the mouth of Blue Creek. This is not the place to go for solitude, however. It's not uncommon to see a hundred or more steelheaders packed into this little area. It's also not uncommon to see a hundred or more steelhead drawn from this stretch of water over the course of a few hours.

I walked the quarter-mile trail from the hatchery to Blue Creek one summer morning. The anglers at the Creek were doing great, mostly with jigs and bobbers, or with bait bounced along the bottom. But crowds rarely suit me. I generally need a little more elbow room, both because I prefer to fish for steelhead with a fly rod . . . and just because.

Moving upstream from Blue Creek, I was able to find water that wasn't too crowded, at least by Cowlitz standards. There is also some bank angling opportunity further upstream below the salmon hatchery's barrier dam, a good spot if you get there in time to stake out a claim to the turf.

There's no doubt about it; you need to be in the right frame of mind to fish the Cowlitz. I usually prefer to fish in more tranquil surroundings, but I'll sometimes stop by the Cowlitz after a day on one of my favorite summer rivers in the vicinity, such as the South Fork Toutle, Green, Kalama, or East Fork Lewis. Sometimes I'm pleasantly surprised to find only a few other anglers there, and I rarely leave without hooking steelhead. There's no denying there are solid reasons for this river's popularity.

Mountain Trout

Waptus Lake, mid-July

It had been nearly 30 years since I'd visited Waptus Lake. As a kid, I'd horse-packed in with my dad and his cowboy brother, my Uncle Perry. All I remember about the fishing is that the rises were too far out in the lake to reach. Later, in my mountain climbing years, I'd viewed Waptus from the high peaks above and thought, *I oughta get back there someday.* When my friend Tim Irish suggested a fishing excursion to Waptus, I jumped at the chance.

It was mid-July when my son, Jordan, and I hiked the 10 miles from Salmon La Sac Campground to Waptus Lake, a journey that took us exactly four hours over an easy trail. We had planned to make the trip in June, but snow postponed our departure a few weeks. When we arrived at the lake, there were still a few snowdrifts beneath the trees.

All we'd had to pack in were our sleeping bags and personal gear. Tim had hired a horse outfitter to haul in the rest of our supplies and equipment. Part of the load was a 14-foot inflatable boat complete with rowing frame—just what we would need to seriously explore and fish this big lake, one of the largest in the Alpine Lake Basin. We arrived at Waptus to a backpacker's fantasy come true: camp had been set up, a cold beer was waiting, and steaks were ready for the grill!

As we finished off the apple pie Tim had baked in his camp oven, fish began rising beyond casting range, just as I remembered from childhood. Only this time, we had a boat. Leaving clean-up for later, we set out to explore.

The shore along the eastern end of the lake had a sandy bottom, gradually sloping and weedless—which explained why all the

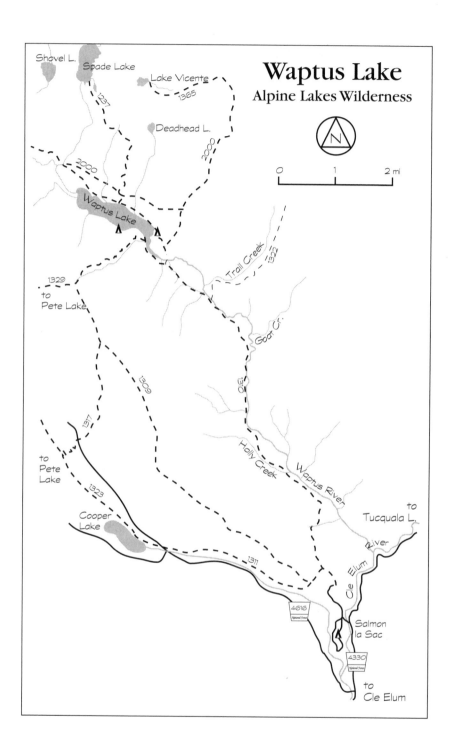

Waptus Lake

Alpine Lakes Wilderness

Shovel L.
Spade Lake
Lake Vicente
1357
1365
Deadhead L.
2000
2000
Waptus Lake
Trail Creek
1322
1329
to
Pete Lake
Goat Cr.
1309
1310
1317
to
Pete
Lake
1323
Holly Creek
Waptus River
Cooper
Lake
to
Tucquala L.
River
Cle Elum
1311
4616
National Forest
Salmon
la Sac
4330
National Forest
to
Cle Elum

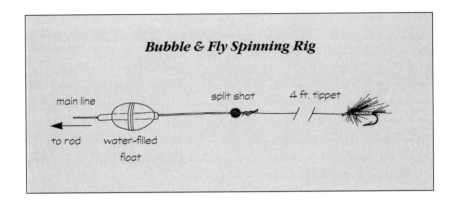

Bubble & Fly Spinning Rig

main line

split shot

4 ft. tippet

to rod

water-filled float

fish were rising farther out. Where we'd seen the fish rising, 30-40 feet from shore, there was an abrupt drop-off. By the time we reached it, surface action had stopped, so we worked the drop-off with small nymphs on sinking-tip fly lines. During the last hours before dark we caught several rainbow, cutthroat, and brook trout. A couple were in the 18-inch range—impressive for mountain trout.

The next day we made a complete circle of the lake, trolling sinking nymphs and streamers behind the raft. The sandy shelf almost encircled the lake, and trees and huckleberry bushes crowded the shoreline. There were few places from which to make an effective cast from shore, at least with a fly rod. But from our raft, Waptus Lake proved to be generous. We took trout all along the drop-off, including several more 18-inchers.

As we completed our circle of the lake in late-afternoon, trout were just beginning to rise again along the edge of the drop-off. This time we were able to see what they were taking: flying black ants. Each time one hit the water, a trout was right on it. We switched to floating lines as fast as we could. I trimmed a few patterns so they could pass for ants, and we were soon hitting a fish with every cast.

Later, back at camp, we found we had neighbors—a couple of guys in a small tent who met us at the shore full of questions, including "How was the fishing?" and "How'd you get all this gear up here?" I confess we led them on a bit, saying we'd packed it all in on our backs. As for the fishing, they pretty much knew. Sound carries well on these high lakes, and they'd been watching us from shore.

Alpine Lakes Wilderness

In the heart of the North Cascades near the geographic center of Washington is a mountain angler's paradise called the Alpine Lakes Wilderness, a basin of over 200 lakes, most of which contain trout. Ranging in size from a few acres to nearly half a square mile, each lake is unique in character and structure, but they all share at least one thing in common: breathtaking alpine scenery.

To appreciate the opportunity here, take a look at a topographic map of the region. Fishing possibilities abound for anglers who don't mind a trek. Some involve only a short hike, while others require a strenuous ascent of several miles and several hundred vertical feet.

The most common trout species found in these lakes are rainbow, cutthroat and brook trout. A few contain the elusive golden trout, including (but not limited to) Ptarmigan (King County), Glacier, Lemah and Three Queens (Kittitas County), and Hidden Lake (North Cascades National Park). Although rare in Washington, grayling can be found in Upper Granite Lake (Skagit County) and have recently been introduced in King's and Marshall lakes (Pend Oreille County).

Access to the basin, which is in the Mt. Baker-Snoqualmie National Forest, is by foot power only. A network of trails leads into the Wilderness from Forest Service roads south from Highway 2, and north from US Interstate 90. A detailed topographic map of the basin, published by Alpine Lakes Protection Society, is available through map dealers or by writing to ALPS, Route 1, Box 890, Ellensburg, WA 98926.

They actually hadn't done badly either. Using spinning rods, they'd been able to reach the drop-off in a few places, taking enough trout on little spinners and spoons to supplement their freeze-dried dinner.

According to WDFW, Waptus Lake has never been stocked with trout. Its rainbow and brook trout migrated through the lake's outlet stream, the Waptus River. This river feeds into the Cle Elum, which eventually joins the Yakima. The lake's cutthroat population probably dates back to a 1930s stocking of lakes higher up the basin. During heavy runoff, cutthroat fingerlings worked their way down to Waptus, where they made themselves at home.

To reach Waptus Lake, follow Trail 1310 from Salmon La Sac Campground on the Cle Elum River four miles north of Cle Elum Lake. For trail conditions, contact the Wenatchee National Forest, Cle Elum Ranger District (509-674-4411).

Spade Lake, early August

Spade Lake, a sliver of blue crystal at elevation 5,050 ft., is a grueling three miles beyond Waptus by way of Trail 1337. I made the trek to 122-acre Spade one summer, spending an idyllic few days casting to its plentiful and willing cutthroat. Giant granite slabs surrounding the lake made casting easy. As with many of these cold, clear gems, Spade looks barren upon first observation. But when you cast a fly or toss a lure, trout materialize out of the depths. In fact, seldom is a lure or fly refused, since food is scarce in the short alpine growing season, and the fish are far more naive about phony food.

On this visit to Spade, in a fit of exploratory enthusiasm, I even made the scramble (there is no trail) from Spade up to Venus Lake, rumored to contain cutthroat. It offered a great view, but was still completely frozen over in mid-July.

When exploring alpine lakes, I always travel light. My usual fishing gear includes a light-weight, four-piece spinning outfit, a handful of assorted tiny spinners and spoons, and a small box of dry flies (Adams, Royal Coachman, flying ant, mosquito). To cast flies with a spinning outfit, attach one of those water-filled bobbers to the line to add the needed weight.

Coldwater Lake, mid-August

When Mt. St. Helens blew its top on May 18, 1980, a landslide on the northwest side of the mountain dammed little Coldwater Creek, adding one more lake to Washington's already generous inventory. Left to nature, the lake might have eventually burst its dam, causing additional havoc downstream. Enter the Army Corps of Engineers. The Corps built an outlet to prevent the earthen dam from breaking, and today Coldwater Lake is stable. Stocked with rainbow trout, it opened to fishing in 1993.

During the summer of 1994, I made the journey up Highway 504 to fish the lake with my boys Luke and Jordan, and my father-in-law, Jack Elefritz. We stopped to view the lake from the Mt. St. Helens Visitor Center on Coldwater Ridge before driving down to the parking area. From above, we were able to spot the shallows, shelves, and the outlet—all important information for the fishing that followed.

Bank fishing at Coldwater is restricted to three designated access points in order to protect the still-fragile shoreline of the new lake. Consequently, most anglers fish Coldwater from float tubes or small boats. (When fishing from a watercraft, you may land only at the designated points.)

After inflating our float tubes, we kicked out to one of the shallows we'd viewed from above and began a slow troll with green and black Woolly Buggers. Immediately, one of the boys was into a fish.

Close by, another angler using a spinning rod and a small spoon had a take. And before either of these were landed, I, too, tied into a fish. Not a bad start!

All three fish were rainbows, and all were about the same size—around 18 inches. Throughout the course of the afternoon we caught and released several more in the same size range. It was obvious that the "one fish over 16-inches" regulation was having its desired effect!

Coldwater does get occasional hatches of caddis and mayflies, and for that reason I always bring a box of dries with me. On this particular visit there were no insect hatches, so we stayed with the Woolly Buggers. Our spinfishing companion switched to a Mepps spinner and had equally good results. We were all fishing single, barbless hooks, as specified by the regulations.

On subsequent trips to Coldwater, I have found a full-sinking line to be the most productive, and I have done best trolling flies very slowly along the bottom. I concentrate my efforts in the obvious shallow areas, which are richest in aquatic insect life and trout.

Although there are both rainbow and cutthroat in Coldwater, I have only caught rainbow. Most of the cutthroat are rumored to be at the north end near the inlet of this long, 700-acre lake—a bit far to kick a tube! In fact, most anglers stick pretty close to the south end of the lake, since all but electric motors are prohibited.

The rainbows were stocked in 1989, and the cutthroat, to everyone's surprise, somehow survived the blast. Both species are now self-sustaining.

While in the Mt. St. Helens area, if you feel both hardy and adventurous, you might give Castle Lake a try. Also in the blast zone, Castle is tough to get to but has produced its share of trout over five pounds, with rumors of eight- and ten-pounders.

Mt. St. Helens Monument maps show trail 221 leading to Castle Lake off Road 8123 (the Sheep Canyon Trailhead). However, most local anglers access the lake by way of a network of logging roads that branch off the South Toutle Road near the community of Toutle.

Though not recommended for the faint of heart (a rough drive over narrow, un-shouldered roads with logging trucks very much in evidence, followed by an extremely steep hike down to Castle), I nevertheless offer you the following series of numbered roads that lead to this access: from the town of Toutle, follow South Toutle Road, then mainline logging road 4100, followed by roads 4200, 4250, and 3000. Road 3000 leads to the ridge top above Castle. There is no sign indicating you're there, but look for a road off 3000 that has a locked gate. Hike this road (which has washed out in several places) or bushwhack the half-mile down to the lake (15 minutes to get down, considerably longer panting back up).

A good map of the Mt. St. Helens National Monument (forest roads and trails, but not including logging roads) is available at Mt. St. Helens National Monument Visitor Centers. To check ahead for road, trail, and fishing conditions, call the Coldwater Visitor Center (360-274-2131).

When venturing into the backcountry, you should always carry a detailed map of the terrain. USGS topographic quadrangle maps allow you to anticipate and prepare for changes in elevation. National Forest maps (Mt. Baker-Snoqualmie or Wenatchee National Forest for the Alpine Lakes Wilderness; Gifford-Pinchot for the Mt. St. Helens area) are useful for road travel, as is the ubiquitous *Washington Atlas and Gazeteer* published by DeLorme.

Sturgeon

Columbia River, late July

When I got a look at the tackle we'd be using I couldn't help wondering, *how fun is this gonna be?* The gear reminded me of charterboat bottom fishing—stiff, heavy rods and big salmon reels loaded with Dacron line.

My fishing buddy, Pinky Freeman, is a long-time sturgeon fisherman. He had been bugging me to go with him for some time, and I finally caved in. Now I was wondering, *Why?*

My lack of enthusiasm must have been evident as we prepared the boat for launch, because Pinky kept saying things like, "Come on Frog." (Frog is my nickname from long ago). "You're gonna like this." Or, "You'll see Frog. . . this is a kick!"

Launching Pinky's boat at a little ramp along Highway 401, just a few miles east of the Megler-Astoria Bridge, we made the quick run out to Pinky's current favorite hole. We could see the bridge and Astoria as we started fishing, and that's about as accurate a description of the spot as I can give. It's a big river.

Regulations require single, barbless hooks for sturgeon fishing in Washington. When Pinky hauled out the hook set-ups and attached them to our lines, I almost choked. They were about the size of my fist.

"Pinky . . . You've got to be kidding!"

"You'll see, Frog. You'll see."

We baited up the giant hooks with sand shrimp (also known as ghost shrimp—incredibly small for the size of the hooks, not to mention the size of the Columbia's sturgeon). While our bait headed toward the bottom, Pinky instructed me to let the fish mouth the bait for a few seconds before setting the hook. Within a few seconds, we

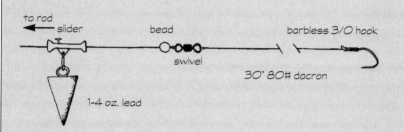

Standard Sturgeon Rig

to rod
slider
bead
barbless 3/O hook
swivel
30" 80# dacron
1-4 oz. lead

Thread the leader through the vent to the mouth so the hook ends up in the bait's mouth. Wrap a few half hitches around the rear half of the bait, leaving only a small amount of leader between the bait and the swivel. (Option: Smear or inject with scent)

Like all fish, sturgeon are found where the food is. For the most part, they are bottom feeders, foraging for shrimp ad whatever other food items they can find among the rocks and sand. Of particular note are those times when anchovies, smelt, or shad are available. Sturgeon become particularly gluttonous then, and some truly monstrous fish can be hooked. Shad are generally in the Columbia mid-May through June; smelt and herring are considerably less predictable.

both had a fish pecking away at our baits One, two, three, four pecks—and I laid into the fish.

I really wasn't prepared for the battle that followed. The sturgeon fought more aggressively than any fish I have ever hooked. Pinky was right. When I brought the sturgeon to the boat, it measured 48 inches—within the legal slot limit (minimum 42 inches, maximum 60) inches. Pinky caught one later that demonstrated what a baby mine was!

Sturgeon can get to be true monsters. Comfortable in both salt and fresh water, some have found their way into freshwater lakes, where they are mistaken for "sea monsters" when they rise to the surface, partially emerge, then sink back down to the depths. Fish weighing several hundred pounds are not uncommon. I once saw an old photo of a Snake River sturgeon that weighed 1,500 pounds.

Sturgeon over 60 inches are considered to be adults and are protected as potential spawners. Great care needs to be taken with these large fish if you happen to hook one. Sturgeon have no skeletal system, so if removed from the water their great weight compresses and strains their internal organs. Big sturgeon should never be removed from the water.

Columbia River sturgeon are being closely studied to insure continuation of the fishery after a near disastrous brush with over-fishing in the early 1900s. For current regulations or information, call the WDFW Columbia River office (360-576-6073).

Naselle River, mid-August

My friend Joe Nelson called one day and asked, "Have you ever caught a sturgeon on a fly?"

The question caught me off-guard. I guess I stammered something like, "Aaah. No."

"Well, do you want to try? I know this place where they're lying on the bottom thick as cord-wood. I've been catching 'em every day."

I had never thought about trying for sturgeon on a fly, but what the heck. We set the trip up for the following morning.

At first light, we were skimming along the road beside Willapa Bay. A light fog cover hung over the water, typical for summer mornings on the coast. The rising sun tinted everything a surrealistic pink. Gulls and snipe were busily feeding on the exposed sand of the receding tide. It was one of those rare mornings that made me glad to be awake and on the road.

A couple miles after crossing the Naselle River on Highway 101, we pulled up to the boat ramp at the Willapa National Wildlife Refuge across from Long Island. We were the only ones there.

Once launched, we headed north, moving at a snail's pace in the fog, since the channel through Long Island Slough is neither wide nor deep. After rounding Stanley Peninsula, it was a clear shot through the mouth of the Naselle and on up the five or so miles to Joe's secret hole.

I'd brought along my heaviest fly rod, a 12-weight. My past encounters with sturgeon had made me a believer in the sheer strength of these critters. Assuming, of course, that they would take a fly.

Joe anchored the boat in a channel about 200-feet wide and 15-feet deep. The tide was still running out at a pretty good pace, but with the 650-grain Teeny Nymph line I was using, I was reasonably sure my fly would reach the bottom.

I tied on a Halfarabbit, one of my favorite flies for lingcod and halibut. Sturgeon feed largely by smell, but I was hoping movement would also be a triggering factor. My 2/0 fly would surely have plenty of that.

Before tying on the fly, I cut my leader back to about two feet. I really didn't think sturgeon would be leader shy, and by using a short leader, I'd be able to keep the fly on the bottom where sturgeon feed.

The Halfarabbit wasn't down ten seconds before a fish picked it up. I set the hook and—nothing! Back down to the bottom, another fish, set the hook...nothing! This went on for several fish. Meanwhile, Joe was hooking, landing, and releasing fish right and left!

I figured I wasn't setting the hook hard enough. Sturgeon have very tough mouths. So when the next fish hit, I was ready. After casting, I pointed my rod tip right at the water. As soon as I felt a fish, I put my whole body weight (hey, careful those of you who know me) into the fish. The battle was on!

Twice during the fight the sturgeon cleared the surface as if shot out of a missile silo. I was having a hoot playing the sturgeon on my long rod, and Joe was having nearly as much fun watching, with an I-told-you-so grin. When the fish came to hand, it was a legal keeper at around 45 inches—not a monster, but significant on a fly rod.

So sturgeon can be taken on a fly rod under certain conditions, though in truth, these conditions are rarely met. The water needs to be shallow, with very little current, as near the mouth of the Naselle. It is also interesting to note that sturgeon don't react to foods entirely by smell.

I should also point out that according to WDFW regulations, sturgeon fishing is allowed only with bait, on single barbless hooks. Fishing with artificial lures is prohibited. I asked a local game warden if fly fishing for them would be OK, and his response was, "Gee, is that possible?" His gut attitude was: "Go ahead and try it, but I doubt you'll catch anything." However, technically, my guess is that flies fall into the prohibited category.

The Columbia River probably offers the best sturgeon fishing in the state, and Bonneville Dam to the mouth is probably the most productive stretch. Bonneville to McNary Dam is also good. The Snake River, Chehalis River, Willapa River and, to a lesser extent, most of the coastal rivers offer good sturgeon fishing near their mouths at times. Commercial sturgeon charters operate out of Ilwaco. For a list of charter operators, contact the Long Beach Chamber of Commerce (360-642-2400).

Stream Trout

Yakima River, early August

I wasn't allowed near the river. It was much too dangerous for a tennis-shoed kid to fish alone. My dad told me about the time a giant whirlpool in the river swallowed a girl and her horse, and how they were never seen again. I don't know whether the story was true or not, but it was enough to make me stay clear. Still, I yearned for the day I could fish the Yakima.

Later, in my teens, I began what was to become a lifelong love affair with the Yakima River. I even wrote a book about it. It is my favorite river, my home water, and I fish it as often as I can, returning to it from my travels with all the eagerness and affection that the term signifies.

Like most rivers, the Yakima has many faces. It begins as the outflow of Keechelus Lake, a big reservoir near Snoqualmie Pass in the Cascade Mountains. It rumbles and tumbles through ranch and farmland down to the Kittitas Valley near Ellensburg, then twists and turns through the great Yakima Canyon—a desert landscape with cactus, rattlesnakes, and less than 10 inches of annual precipitation. Then it waters a rich agricultural area from the city of Yakima to the Tri-Cities (Richland, Pasco, Kennewick) before emptying into the Columbia.

Tim Irish was the Yakima River's first guide. In fact, he was probably Washington State's first trout guide. As recently as the 1980s, a lot of people thought he was foolish to start a guide business that focused on Yakima trout. *Who'd pay to do that?* Boy, how times have changed.

Tim doesn't guide on the river anymore, but we have fished it many times together. Much of that fishing has been during the sum-

The Yakima Canyon's largest rainbows are often within inches of the bank.

mer months when the river is high and moving at too fast a pace for many anglers,

Unlike most rivers, the Yakima is at its fullest in summer, when water is released from mountain reservoirs for irrigation purposes. (The Yakima is responsible for much of the agricultural life of central and south central Washington.)

The first time I floated the river on a serious summer fishing trip was with Tim, and I learned a lot. We launched Tim's raft at the

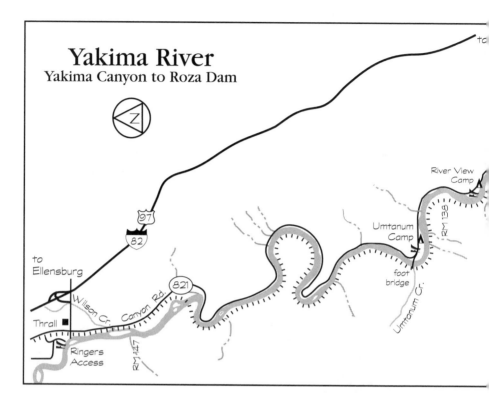

Yakima River
Yakima Canyon to Roza Dam

to

River View Camp

RM 138

Umtanum Camp

foot bridge

Umtanum Cr.

to Ellensburg

Thrall ■

Wilson Cr.

Canyon Rd.

RM 147

Ringers Access

Bighorn launch (now closed) just inside the Yakima Canyon. It was a hot summer day, typical summer weather for the canyon.

Tim had been fishing the river so much, he knew where many of its big rainbows were holding. By big, I mean those in the 18- to 20-inch range—not monsters by some standards, but big for the Yakima.

When we started our float, Tim instructed me to cast my caddis imitation within two inches of the overhanging grass along the river bank as we floated along.

"Five inches out is too far" he said. "Unless you want to catch dinks!"

It took awhile to get the hang of floating my fly drag-free that close to shore, but Tim was right. Whenever I got a decent drift tight against the overhanging vegetation, I would hook a good fish. If my fly drifted out from the bank, when a fish did hit, it was nearly

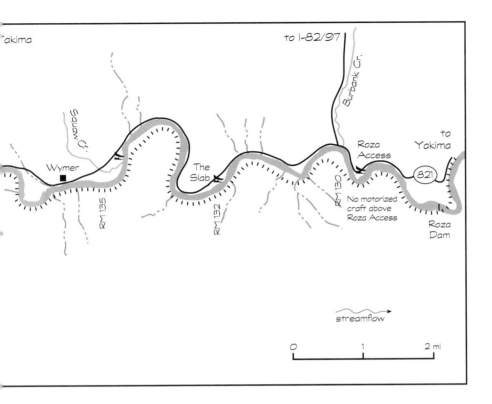

always a small one. The large trout hang out in the cool shadows of overhanging vegetation and wait for food to come to them.

Floating and fishing in this manner requires hundreds of casts during the course of the day. Due to the currents just out from shore, you seldom get a drag-free drift more than a few feet, and your fly must float drag-free or you won't catch many fish.

The best fishing in the Yakima River is the 48-river mile stretch between the towns of Cle Elum (a few miles north of Ellensburg) and Selah (just north of Yakima).

Between Cle Elum and Ellensburg, fewer truly large trout are hooked than in the canyon below, but many anglers prefer this stretch because it sees less pressure than the canyon. A popular float in this section is from the mouth of the Teanaway River down to the diversion dam, a distance of approximately 10 miles. The river here is narrower and faster, and there is less overhanging vegetation along the banks than in the canyon. Highway 10 follows the river throughout this stretch, and there are several wide spots in the road where bank anglers can pull over and gain access to the river.

Just south of Ellensburg, the river enters its 12-mile canyon, a popular stretch noted for very large trout. Floating is unquestionably the best way to cover the water in summer, as the river is at its highest due to irrigation releases at the dams. From June through August, high water limits bank fishing opportunities and makes for tricky wading. Most bank angling in the canyon is done in the fall when the river is easy to wade, from around the second week in September on. Highway 821, which parallels the river all the way to Selah, offers easy bank access throughout the canyon.

The most popular float in the canyon is from Ringers Access to Umtanum Access (about five miles). Another very popular drift is from Umtanum to Squaw Creek (about five miles), or for a longer drift, to "The Slab" (about eight miles). Bighorn Access, mentioned in my book, *Yakima River*, is no longer open.

I once floated the stretch of river from Ellensburg down to the Yakima Canyon entrance. The fishing was fantastic, but the float was life threatening. I have since concluded that this stretch of river really shouldn't be floated. There are too many channels, sweepers, and log jams to deal with. And there are no access points in this stretch. On my one and only float through this section, we ended up carrying our raft a mile or so across a potato field after we abandoned the float out of fear for our lives.

The Yakima is one of Washington's "Selective Fisheries," which means catch and release on artificial flies and lures with barbless hooks. Fly fishing is the most popular technique here—and also the most effective way to fool this river's trout. Caddis are abundant throughout the summer, and trout are almost always willing to take a dark size-14 Elk Hair Caddis. Another favorite summer pattern is a big ol' grasshopper fly fished near the bank. When the hoppers are out, fishing here can be fast and furious. Small spoons and spinners (with single, barbless hooks) are used with success in some of the deeper pools in the upper river.

Whether using fly gear or spinning tackle, a light to medium outfit is all you need. My preference is a five- or six-weight fly rod, floating line, and a nine-foot leader tapered to 4X. A short leader is easier to control than a longer leader when fishing close to the bank.

For information about boat ramps and river hazards, see *Recreational Users' Map of The Yakima River*, published by Kittitas County Field & Stream Club (PO Box 522, Ellensburg, WA 98926). For an in-depth study of the river, take a look at my own *River Journal: Yakima River*, published by Frank Amato Publications. Both are available in most fly shops.

Camping facilities and RV hook-ups near the river are available at a KOA campground at the west I-90 interchange and at River View campground, 15 miles south of Ellensburg on Highway 821. There are public campgrounds at the Umtanum and River View accesses. Camping is also permitted throughout the Yakima Canyon, though there are no developed campgrounds and no facilities in this stretch. Be advised that car break-ins are a problem everywhere along the Yakima. It's best not to leave valuables in your car.

Guide services can be arranged through The Evening Hatch (509-574-8334), and through Coopers Fly Shop, (509-962-5259), both in Ellensburg.

Other good summer trout streams in Washington include the Twisp, Entiat, Methow, Kettle, Colville and Pend Oreille Rivers, all in the north or northeast portion of the state. The Colville and Pend Oreille rivers offer the patient angler a shot at catching a trophy brown trout.

Bass

Potholes Reservoir, mid-August

A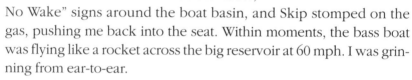nticipation of the ride must have been all over my face, like ice cream "sticky" on a kid.

"First time, huh?" Skip asked.

"Yup" I replied.

About that time we cleared the "Slow, No Wake" signs around the boat basin, and Skip stomped on the gas, pushing me back into the seat. Within moments, the bass boat was flying like a rocket across the big reservoir at 60 mph. I was grinning from ear-to-ear.

Potholes Reservoir filled in the 1950s with the construction of O'Sullivan Dam on Crab Creek. This big (25,000 acres) reservoir in central Washington turned an arid landscape into one of the state's wealthiest agricultural areas. It also created one of Washington's best fisheries. Largemouth bass are one of the 19 warmwater species that thrive here.

Flying low held the 95-degree air temperature temporarily in check as we skimmed the glassy surface, heading for "the dunes" at the north end of the lake. This area is named for the huge sand hills that emerge from the reservoir when it is drawn down for agricultural purposes. As we approached the dunes, Skip throttled back a bit— not quite as much as I would have, but he had done this a million times. I held on a little tighter as we wound our way through a maze of narrow channels and willow-covered sand hills. I wondered how we would ever find our way out.

Deep within the dunes, Skip killed the big engine and dropped the electric trolling motor over the bow. Keeping just within casting distance, we worked our top-water baits close to the willow-choked bank.

Fishing with a guide who is on the water every day certainly has its advantages on big water like Potholes. Its complex submerged structure and wildly varying depths makes finding fish the biggest challenge. Skip knew exactly where to go.

As we moved slowly along the bank, Skip was the first to make contact with a bass. Fishing top-water baits is exciting business, especially when the water explodes the moment a bait touches down. That was the case with this fish. When the largemouth came to hand, Skip said it was an average Potholes bass, around two and a half pounds. Bass to 10 pounds have been taken here, though, and there are enough five-pounders to keep things interesting.

We continued working the banks in different parts of the dunes, picking up the occasional bass. According to Skip, fishing was a bit slow, but then we were fishing mid-day in blazing sun with top-water baits. I was amazed we caught anything at all.

Since that time I have fished with Skip on several occasions,

Crankbaits work well when fishing for bass over submerged structure.

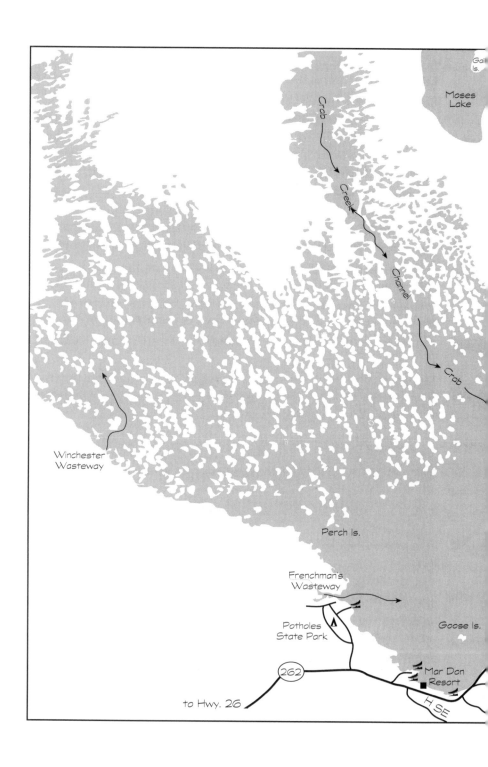

Potholes Reservoir

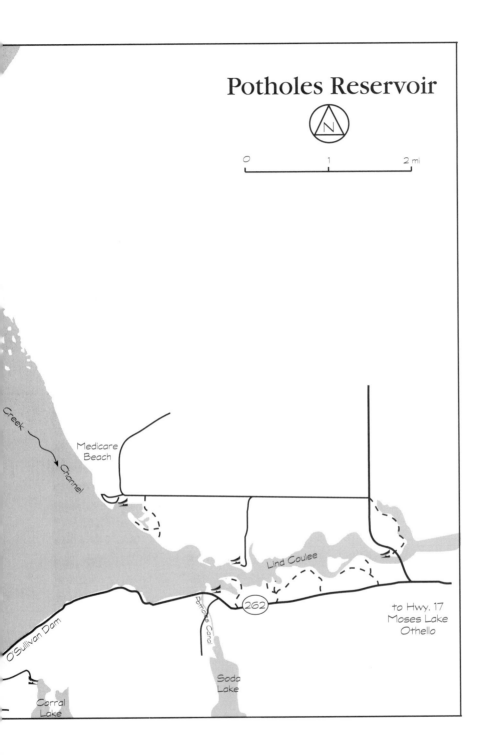

N

0   1   2 mi

Creek

Channel

Medicare
Beach

Lind Coulee

262

to Hwy. 17
Moses Lake
Othello

Potholes Canal

O'Sullivan Dam

Soda
Lake

Corral
Lake

Potholes Bass Tips

Good bass water is typically near some kind of structure—because that's where the food is. On Potholes, structure can be an underwater rise in the lake bottom, rock piles, vegetation (willows, reeds, lily pads), sunken beaver dams, docks, points of land, or along the face of the dam, among others. Each of these is fished in a different manner and with different baits.

Top-water baits are very good in warm water situations over shallow, weedy areas and along shorelines. When twitched and jerked across the surface, these baits can produce explosive takes. Among the most popular at Potholes are Rebel's Super Pop-R and the Johnson Floating Minnow. For fly fishers, hair poppers serve the same purpose and are effective.

When fishing over rock piles or other sunken structure, plastic worms, spinnerbaits and crankbaits work best. Try varying your depth until you begin hitting fish. Rapala's Rattlin' Fat Rap, Storm's Thunderstick, and Cabela's Triple Take Spinnerbaits are good choices.

When fishing heavy vegetation or over sunken timber, Texas-style worms and Jig & Pig combos work very well when worked slowly around and over the structure.

and I have learned a lot about the reservoir. For example, the most consistently productive fishing seems to be near the mouths of the three inlets: Frenchman and Winchester wasteways on the west side, and Crab Creek in the northeast corner.

Since there is such a variety of water, all sorts of methods, tackle, and baits are appropriate here. For the excitement of the take, crankbaits and top-water plugs are my favorite hard baits, but plastic worms, jigs, and basically any bait works as well. My very favorite way to fish Potholes Reservoir is with a fly rod and hair poppers, but this is most effective during early morning and late evening.

Steve Potter and I were high school buddies. However, it wasn't until fifteen years later, when we were both making a living in the fishing business, that we first fished together. I heard he was guiding on Potholes Reservoir, and when I got a magazine assignment to do a fly-rodding for bass article, I called Steve and booked a trip for an evening in July. Our plan was to fish until dark, casting hair poppers over some of Steve's favorite water.

It was hot as I drove east from Royal City on Highway 26 towards Potholes, typical summer weather in eastern Washington. Giant, self propelled sprinkler systems were watering the fields. Beyond the reach of the sprinklers, the earth was parched and brown.

I followed the signs to Mar Don Resort, which brought me right to the reservoir. I was to meet my old friend Steve at the Mar Don store.

I loaded my gear into Steve's bass boat, and we headed across the lake towards Crab Creek. Waiting for the sun to sink lower in the western sky, we caught up on old times. We didn't want to fish any of Steve's favorite spots until the sun was just right—no sense spooking the fish. When the sun finally disappeared behind the hills, Steve jockeyed the boat into position, and we began punching casts into the shoreline.

We were fishing areas where small willows protruded from the water, our hair frog "flies" twitching only inches from shore. Fishing till dark, we caught countless bass. It was the best evening of bass fishing I have ever had.

In addition to largemouth bass, Potholes Reservoir is a top producer of smallmouth bass, walleye, rainbow trout, and some of the largest crappie and perch I have ever seen.

Fishing from a boat is pretty much required on the big reservoir, with a few exceptions. There are times when fishing along the face of the dam can be exceptional, and you can walk the rocks the entire distance. I have taken some very nice rainbow trout and smallmouth bass from the dam face, especially near the outlet of

Potholes Canal. Crappie fishing off the dock at Mar Don Resort can be fantastic.

While in the area, I like to spend time on a few other nearby lakes. Soda and Long lakes are connected to Potholes Reservoir by way of Potholes Canal. These lakes contain the same species of fish as Potholes, and are a good bet on those windy days when the Reservoir kicks up and is dangerous for small boats.

There are a many other lakes in the immediate vicinity, including the seep lakes to the south (See map p. 160). A small cartop boat, float tube, or even bank fishing are options on these lakes.

Mar Don Resort (509-765-5061) at the southwest corner of Potholes Reservoir is the best source for current information on fishing conditions throughout the area. Resort facilities include a motel, shaded campground, boat ramp, fishing dock, store, and restaurant. There is also camping and a public boat ramp at Potholes State Park at the south end of the lake, and another public ramp at Lind Coulee (a long arm of water which reaches east from the south end of the reservoir). As for guides, I can highly recommend Skip Davis (509-349-8004).

A word of caution: this is snake country. Step carefully, and keep an eye out when tromping along the banks.

Silver Lake, early September

There were three or four bass boats, all decked out and glittery, ahead of our econo model: a 12-foot aluminum job with a six-horse Evinrude. No fancy swivel seats here; I sat on the ice chest. Still, Pinky and I were as happy as a couple of clams  at high tide when we slipped his boat into Silver Lake on this misty September morning.

We chugged across the lake, heading towards the southern shore. I don't know why we were headed for the southern shore;

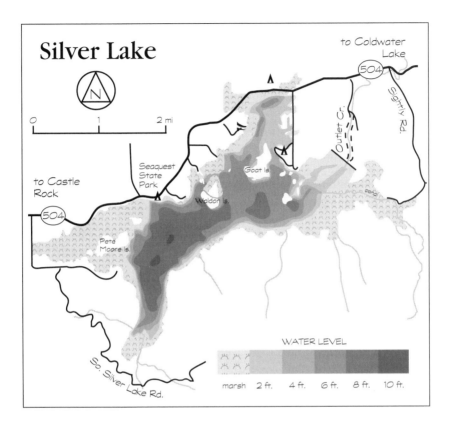

Silver Lake

to Coldwater Lake

504

Sightly Rd.

Outlet Cr.

to Castle Rock

504

Seaquest State Park

Goat Is.

Waldon Is.

Pete Moore Is.

WATER LEVEL

marsh   2 ft.   4 ft.   6 ft.   8 ft.   10 ft.

So. Silver Lake Rd.

0   1   2 mi

the whole lake looks the same. It is a shallow lake, rarely over seven feet deep, and the entire perimeter is plastered with a thick lily pad cover.

When the floating green carpet on the far side came within range, Pinky killed the motor, and we drifted in silence to the edge of the pads. At least, we were as silent as you can be in an aluminum boat.

On this day, Pinky and I were both fly fishing. I was using a big hair popper. Pinky had knotted on a large, eel-type pattern, which looked very much like a plastic worm when in the water. Both of our flies were tied weedless, with a monofilament guard protecting the hook—a necessity when fishing this weed-choked lake.

We cast our creations right into the lily jungle and, just like on those TV bass shows, largemouth bass came charging out of the

Tying the Weedless Hair Popper

Hook: Daiichi 2720 size 2- to 5/0

Tail: 4 saddle hackles, rubber leg strips

Hackle: 2 saddle hackles

Body: Spun and clipped deer hair

Legs: Rubber leg material

Eyes: Plastic Doll eyes

Step 1: Secure a piece of 25 lb. stiff monofilament to the hook shank and leave protruding behind the bend of the hook. It will be used in a later step.

Step 2: Tie in 4 saddle hackles and a couple of rubber strands for the tail.

Step 3: Wind on 2 large saddle hackles at the butt of the fly.

Step 4: Spin deer hair around the hook shank, tying in two sets of rubber legs, mid-body.

Step 5: Trim deer hair into the classic popper shape.

Step 6: Glue Doll eyes to deer hair with 5-min. epoxy.

Step 7: Bring monofilament forward and secure at eye of hook to form the weed guard. Finish head and cement to complete the fly.

pads and took our offerings like there'd be no tomorrow. We couldn't keep the four-pound bass off our lines. The next trip I made to Silver Lake I got skunked.

Washington has many little waters just waiting to be fished.

Shallow Silver Lake yields largemouth bass.

Float tubes are ideal for fishing high mountain lakes.

Yakima River rainbow.

Bass are more fickle than most fish, and Silver Lake bass are moody even by bass standards. I get skunked on half my trips here—or at least often enough that I remember the details of the last time. I've heard Silver Lake old timers complain of this same lockjaw problem, so I know it isn't just me.

On the other hand, Silver Lake hands over enough very nice largemouth bass to keep me coming. In fact, the regulations set the minimum keeper size at 14 inches, which says something about the standards here. I have been on Silver Lake during the spring spawn, and some of the bass I saw in the shallows were downright scary.

One of the things that attracts me to Silver Lake is the fact that it is shallow, and top-water baits (my favorite) work almost any time. They are especially effective in summer when the bass move from the shallows into the comparatively deeper, more open water (where you don't have to worry about a hang-up).

When fishing the heavily vegetated areas of the lake, weedless baits are the only way to go. Still, I prefer top-water weedless baits, such as floating weedless spoons and buzz baits. That's just a personal preference, of course, and any of the popular bass baits will work if fished properly . . . if the fish are in the mood to feed.

Three large islands and the irregular, heavily vegetated shore-line of Silver Lake offer fantastic habitat not only for largemouth bass, but for crappie, bluegill, perch, and catfish, which are all present in abundance.

Cupped within the broad Toutle River valley, Silver Lake was formed as a result of one of Mt. St. Helens' earlier eruptions. During the last major eruption in 1980, there was fear that the lake would be washed away by the raging Toutle, but fortunately it was spared.

To reach Silver, take State Route 504 east from I-5. The highway follows the northern lake shore, but there are only three access points. The first, at the west end, is a little tackle/boat rental shop. I always stop here and ask where the action is and what they're hitting. There's a public boat ramp about mid-lake, and another boat ramp at the east end of the lake.

Seaquest State Park near the west end of the lake offers a large campground (70 campsites), nature trails, and day use facilities. A short trail leads from the park to the Mount St. Helens Visitor Center, across Highway 504.

Potholes and Silver Lake are just two of Washington's many productive bass waters. Moses Lake, Roosevelt Lake, and Banks Lake on the eastside, and Seattle's Lake Washington on the westside are also extremely productive. And there are dozens and dozens more. Because of our historical fascination with salmon, steelhead, and trout, most of these waters are underfished. Eastside bass fisheries get the heaviest pressure, but many of these waters are big enough to absorb a lot of anglers without feeling crowded—or making a dent in the bass population.

Little Ponds and Creeks

My son, Jordan, a hopeless fishing addict like his dad, recently had me drop him off with two of his buddies, Mitch and Aaron, at a little pond on state land beside a stand of timber a few miles out of Raymond, where we live. They had no idea what they would find there, if anything. As it turned out, they all caught a few decent bass. Now they fish this little pond a couple times a week, riding their bikes out to it, or hitching a ride with one or another of us parents.

After leaving the boys at their pond that first day, I was reminded of my own boyhood fishing experiences, which are among the most vivid from my lifetime as an angler. I particularly remembered a little meadow stream near my home. Mint and wild iris grew tall in the meadow, filling the day with color and the air with a wonderful fragrance. Woodpeckers hammered away at the giant cottonwoods streamside. As I looked back, the scene was postcard perfect. But I didn't notice it then; that's not why I was there. Nope, I was there for the trout!

They weren't big trout. I suppose the largest was maybe 10 or 12 inches. And I measured countless little trout to see if they were

Wherever you live in Washington, there is a little stream or pond capable of yielding hours of fishing pleasure close to home.

legal keepers. I could pretty much count on catching at least one fish out of every good hole. And I knew all the good holes. I fished that little creek a lot.

When I ran out of worms, and I always did when the fishing was good, I chased grasshoppers around the meadow, bringing them back one by one until my wild hopper catching put me face to face with a snake, as it inevitably did. They were always garter snakes, but I knew there were rattlesnakes around, so any snake would send me back to digging worms.

I didn't play fish back then. The instant I got a bite, I flung the fish to shore. If it was too big to fling, it broke off. It never occurred to me there was another way. Remembering, I shook my head, amazed that 35 years had passed since I last fished that meadow stream.

Wherever you live in Washington, there is a little stream or pond close by. It's one of the characteristics of the state. When I was growing up, I had half a dozen such waters I would fish regularly. The only limit on my fishing was how far I was willing to pedal my bicycle that day. And I rarely encountered another angler on my water. Some of those waters are gone now, victims of urban development or natural processes. But Washington is full of similar little waters just waiting to be fished.

Finding small creeks and ponds is easy. You'll pass over many a creek while driving the state's country roads, or see a pond glistening off in a field or through a stand of trees. You can also study a USGS topographic map for the quadrant in which you live, noting streams and ponds; then compare the map with a county road map or DeLorme's *Washington Atlas and Gazeteer* to figure out how to get from here to there. You'll find that most of these little waters are on private property, so ask permission before you fish. Just knock on the nearest door and ask. In all my life of fishing such waters, I have only been denied permission to fish a couple of times.

As we grow older and have the means to get to the larger, more notable rivers and lakes in pursuit of larger quarry, we tend to forget about the little waters. That's our loss. Many of these little creeks and ponds are perfect miniatures of the bigger models, each with its own character, structure, whims, and challenges. Each is worth investigating, capable of yielding surprises and many hours of pleasure. And best of all, they're close to home.

Night Fishing

Dry Falls Lake, early September

The sun had set, but the air temperature was still 85 degrees. As we blew up our float tubes, the last fisherman on the lake rowed to shore. I walked over to help him hoist his small boat into the back of his pickup.

"How was fishing?" I asked.

"Worst day I have ever had on this lake!" was his reply. "Only hooked three fish all afternoon, and none of them were worth writing home about!"

Then came a barrage of questions.

"How come you guys are just heading out now?"

"How can you see in the dark?"

"Ever see any snakes in the water?"

I answered as best I could, but when he drove off, I'm sure he thought we were a loony bunch.

It was nearly dark when we entered the water. By the time we quit fishing, we had each landed and released a couple dozen fat trout from a lake that probably hadn't give up that many fish throughout that entire summer day to all its anglers combined.

Contrary to popular wisdom, fish do not stop feeding when the water reaches summer high temperatures. If anything, since their metabolism picks up when it's warm, fish feed more voraciously than usual. But they do most of their feeding at night.

Some larger fish feed almost exclusively under the protective cover of darkness. This is especially true of big brown trout. I have night-hooked large browns in desert lakes that produced only small rainbows during the day.

Tying the Night Leech

Hook: TMC 300 size 6 or 4

Thread: Black monocord

Tail: Black marabou

Body: Black ESTAZ

Hackle: Black pheasant rump

Wing: Black bunny strip

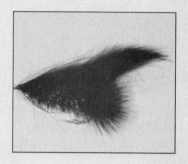

Step 1: Tie in a tail of black marabou. Leave a 10-inch piece of thread at the butt of the fly to be used in a later step.

Step 2: Secure a piece of black ESTAZ to hook and wind forward to form the body.

Step 3: Tie in a piece of dyed black rabbit strip at the head of the fly.

Step 4: Pull the fur towards the butt, and with the thread left at the butt of the fly, wind forward securing the fur Zonker-style to the top of the body. To avoid smashing the fur down with the thread, wet your fingers and stand the hair fibers up before winding the thread forward.

Step 5: Tie in the pheasant rump feather by the tip.

Step 6: Wind the hackle two turns and secure. Trim the rabbit fur strip so that it extends to the length of the marabou. Finish head and cement to complete the Night Leech.

But night fishing is not for everyone. There are risks to consider, and everything you do is harder because you really can't see very well. But neither can the fish, and that kind of evens things out!

All but a handful of Washington waters are open 'round-the-clock.

What do fish see at night? Fish can see a silhouetted fly or lure very well in the darkness. In addition, they will tune into the sound of your offering moving through the water. For this reason I always use big lures for night fishing—size 4, 3XL, and size 2, 3XL when fly fishing—because they make a lot of noise, both when they touch down and when retrieved.

I only use two fly patterns for nighttime fishing. My favorite, which I designed, is the Night Leech. This is a big (three or four inches long) leech imitation tied with dyed black rabbit fur, and is similar to some of the commercial leech patterns available. Using a leader no longer than four feet tapered to 1X, I cast it on a floating line, working over shallow weedbeds and along shorelines. Slowly retrieving this pattern gets a lot of attention from the big boys.

The other fly I use at night is a big mouse pattern. I fish it on a sinking-tip line, casting it tight against the shore. If a big trout or bass is close by, it will pounce on the mouse as soon as it touches down. If nothing happens, I let the fly sit motionless and allow the sinking tip to settle. Then I make a quick, long strip which causes the fly to dive under sharply and make a "plop" as it breaks the surface. This commotion draws fish like a magnet.

I have found that the darker the night, the better the fishing. If there is a full moon I rarely bother going out. One night, I was fishing Lenice Lake under a bright moon. Fishing was slow. There were small patches of fluffy clouds passing overhead, and when one passed in front of the moon—bingo! The fish turned on. When the cloud cleared the moon—slow again. A new cloud—fish on again. And so on throughout the night.

I can't emphasize enough that, if you fish at night, you must keep safety issues in mind. You should only fish water that you know well, use barbless hooks, wear a life jacket, and by all means, carry a dependable flashlight.

If you're fly fishing, don't make long casts. It's just plain dangerous, both for you and for others close by. And there is no need to cast long. The trout can't see you, so you won't spook them by casting close. I rarely cast out more than 20 feet at night, which allows me to maintain control over my cast and know where my fly is at all times.

Night fishing isn't everyone's idea of a fun time, but if you can handle the frustrations and are interested in fast action and trophy trout, you might give it a try.

All but a handful of Washington waters are open for round-the-clock fishing, but check the rule book for the water you choose just to be certain. My favorite choices for night fishing are the trout lakes of central Washington, but virtually all Washington lake fisheries can be productive on summer nights.

Fall

For anglers in other parts of the country, autumn marks the beginning of the end, and they approach it with wistfulness and dread of the fishless months ahead. But here in the Pacific northwest where the fishing season is endless, autumn is more like a new beginning.

Fall chinook and searun cutthroat head in from the ocean. Desert trout shake themselves out of their late summer torpor. And these are in addition to the summer fisheries—bottomfish, steelhead, sturgeon, and stream trout— which continue undiminished throughout the fall.

Autumn is my favorite season. Its crisp days bring everything into sharp focus and intensify the colors of the season—the vibrant red vine maples, the brilliant yellow alders. Even spider webs emerge from their usual anonymity and sparkle like jewels on dewy autumn mornings as I walk to the little cutthroat stream near my home.

There's also an urgency in the air, a sense that this won't last. These beautiful days will soon give way to winter rains. *Do it now* becomes the operational refrain. *It* being fishing, of course. Everything else that needs doing can wait.

Desert Lakes Come Alive Again

Mid-September

In the heat of summer, many of Washington's desert lakes grow so warm that their oxygen content thins. Resident trout become lethargic and unresponsive until the comparatively cooler hours of darkness. Because of this, most anglers by-pass the desert lakes in summer in favor of more productive fisheries.

But by mid-September, though days are still warm, desert nights are cool enough to lower water temperature around the clock. For anglers, it's as if the desert lakes awaken from a months-long sleep. Once again, as in spring, trout can be found cruising throughout the day, gorging themselves on the abundant forage and willing to try almost anything that looks edible.

Fall also offers desert anglers a few pleasant bonuses: daytime temperatures are mild rather than hot; there are considerably fewer anglers on the water; and the wind, almost incessant in spring, is more sporadic.

Lenice Lake, late September

If you didn't know Lenice Lake was just a half-mile down the trail, you wouldn't have a clue there was water within a hundred miles. The soft, sun-baked sand tugs at your feet as you climb the dunes. Progress seems dream-like, as if you're  moving in slow motion. The tawny grass has waved lifeless in the sun and wind for months, and the only hint of green is the gray-green of sagebrush, which isn't picky about not having a lot to drink.

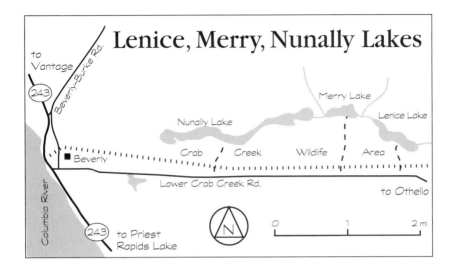

Lenice, Merry, Nunally Lakes

to Vantage

Beverly-Burke Rd.

243

Merry Lake

Nunally Lake

Lenice Lake

Crab / Creek   Wildlife / Area

Beverly

Lower Crab Creek Rd.

to Othello

Columbia River

243 to Priest
Rapids Lake

N

0   1   2 mi

Located in central Washington just east of the Columbia River, Lenice is one of a string of spring-fed lakes near Crab Creek. To reach it, follow Highway 243 to the little community of Beverly. At Beverly, follow the main road east through town toward Crab Creek Wildlife Area. In about five miles, you will come to a small, well-marked parking lot.

When I was growing up, I heard stories of Lenice's fabulous trout and looked forward to fishing it myself one day. My first trip there was with my dad, on a sunny fall afternoon. The lake was calm, with only a scattered dozen or so float tubes and a single canoe in sight. I planned to fish from a tube, while my dad would wade out from shore.

I tied on a small Gold Ribbed Hare's Ear Nymph—my favorite searching pattern. Kicking out from shore, I trolled my fly using an intermediate line, the slowest of the sinking lines. I moved parallel to the shoreline, out far enough that I could just make out the bottom.

I had been fishing about ten minutes when I hooked my first Lenice Lake rainbow. I was amazed at its strength and endurance. Typical of desert trout, this 18-inch fish had an enormous girth, testimony to the abundant food supply in desert lakes. I admired, photographed, and released the trout for grins another day.

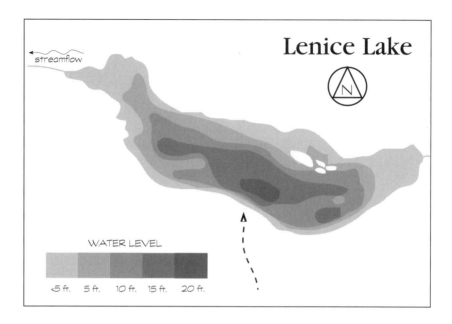

Almost immediately after I released the rainbow, a wind raced across the desert out of the west. I heard it roar moments before it hit with a staggering force. Within seconds, I heard a loud clap from the middle of the lake, then screams muffled by the wind blast. A canoe had capsized with such force that it's impact with the water sounded like a rifle shot. A couple of tubers went to the rescue and helped the cold duo to shore. Dad and I left. It was quite an introduction to Lenice Lake—its productivity and its autumn bluster!

Over the years, I have often returned to Lenice Lake. It is one of my favorite desert fisheries, and despite the dramatic initiation, there are far fewer windy days here in fall than in spring.

Under Selective Fishery Regulations, both flies and lures with single barbless hooks are allowed at Lenice. However, fly angling is the most effective method for fishing here.

During the fall there are few insect hatches other than midges, but beneath the surface there are legions of damselfly and dragonfly nymphs, leeches, scuds, and the larval or nymphal stage of all the insects that hatched earlier in the year.

Two other lakes, Merry and Nunnally, are connected to Lenice by a small stream. Though not as widely known or popular as Lenice, both are productive and can be fished similarly. Trails lead directly to these lakes from parking areas along Crab Creek Road.

All three of these lakes have wadeable shorelines, an uncommon attribute among Washington's desert lakes, which generally tend to steep banks and soft, muddy shores. Unfortunately, poaching is especially prevalent here due to the easy bank access and remoteness. Citizen help is appreciated. To report violations, call Washington's poaching hotline (800-477-6224).

Dusty Lake, early October

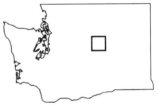

My pack must have weighed 60 pounds. That's heavy, but I have packed more. Back in my mountain climbing days, a 60-pound pack was a normal load to haul into base camp. But on this particular occasion, I was not only carrying the heavy pack, I was also riding a mountain bike down a rough, rock-covered trail.

A dozen of us were heading for Dusty Lake, near Quincy in central Washington, planning to spend a few days and nights in pursuit of the lake's hefty rainbow and brown trout. After a couple of miles on the back-breaking, rear-pounding trail (actually an old road, closed to motor vehicles and leading right to the lake), we reached our destination.

Like many of the lakes in the volcanic central Columbia Basin, Dusty is surrounded by basalt cliffs. The only open area is on the west shore, and it didn't take us long to assemble a cozy little camp there, blow up our float tubes, and hit the water.

Our campsite fronted on a small, shallow bay. The lake was calm, and we could see fish rising. Nothing obvious was hatching, so we each picked our favorite fly and worked over the weedbeds

A rough access road keeps the pressure low and the average catch size high at Dusty Lake.

that covered much of the bay. Woolly Buggers, Gold Ribbed Hare's Ear Nymphs, and various leech patterns took most of the fish. It was a productive afternoon.

There is no access into Dusty other than the old road and a steep trail that winds down the cliffs on the east end of the lake. For this reason, Dusty gets less pressure than do drive-in lakes in the basin. Still, Dusty has a faithful following. Most anglers on this day were fishing from the east shore, having come in on the trail rather than the road. We had the west end of the lake to ourselves.

One of the things I was looking forward to was fishing for browns at night. Dusty is known to have some real lunkers. We planned to fish the shallows every night of our stay in hopes of nailing a trophy. Unfortunately, the weather deteriorated after our first night. We awoke to a strong wind, a wind more characteristic of an eastern Washington spring. Enthusiasm dwindled as we cast between the gusts, and after a discouraging hour, we packed up and left.

The following week, I had to go out of town, but my friends returned to Dusty. The weather was beautiful, and they caught monster browns all night long. Oh well . . .

Chopaka Lake, mid-October

Long before I made my first journey to eastern Washington's Chopaka Lake, I'd heard horror stories about the godawful road that leads to this famous fly-fishing-only trout lake near the little town of Loomis, not far from the Canadian border.  Now I was experiencing it first hand, and I appreciated my car's front wheel drive as I headed up the steep grade. Snow, mud, or even meeting another car would be more than exciting. But I made it to the lake without incident.

Chopaka covers 160 acres and sits in a small bowl, surrounded on three sides by arid, pine-covered hills. The fourth side, the south, features an outlet and the approach road. When I arrived, there were a half-dozen float tubers on the water. It was late in the day, and as I was hoping, an evening hatch was in progress. I built my camp in record time, got ready to fish, and launched my float tube.

Chopaka Lake was first stocked with trout in the early 1950s, and since it was a long way from everywhere, it didn't get much pressure. The handful of anglers who fished it caught rainbows averaging three pounds, and slightly smaller cutthroat. After access to the lake was "improved," the catch limit remained the same, and consequently the average size of the catch went down.

At first the Game Department tried replenishing the lake with Atlantic salmon, but that experiment failed here as elsewhere in the state. Thereafter, the Game Department concentrated on trout, planting fewer and regulating more strictly. With its current one-fish daily bag limit, Chopaka has come back in a big way.

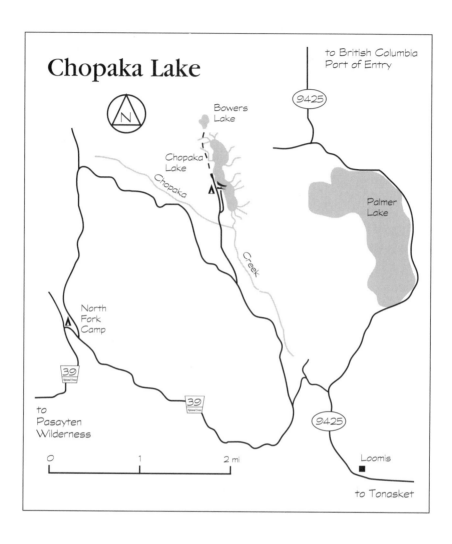

At elevation 2,900 feet, the lake stays cold enough, and gets enough moisture, to provide good fishing throughout its open season (April through October). Many anglers consider it to be Washington's best dry fly lake. Mayflies and/or caddis hatches occur throughout the season, with mayflies more prevalent in spring and summer, and caddis providing a good show in the fall. As I kicked my tube out into the lake on that first trip, it was the caddis the trout were rising to.

I eased away from shore, knotting on a size 12 Elk Hair Caddis,

Fishing the Traveling Sedge

The angler who witnesses a hatch of caddis on stillwater is in for a treat indeed—providing that angler has a few caddis imitations in the fly box.

The large traveling sedge (caddis), best known in the lakes of British Columbia, emerges at midday, hatching well into the darkness of night. The adults run erratically on the water, leaving a wake as they head for shore. There are several sub-species, and adults can range from a quarter inch to one and a half inches in length. Their bodies are shades of browns and greens, with wings of beige, brown, gray, or mottled combinations.

The imitation should be presented on a floating line, skated and twitched across the surface just like the naturals. Cast out and let the fly sit motionless for a few seconds, then start a fast, continuous retrieve for a couple of feet. Let the fly sit motionless again for a few seconds, give it a couple of twitches, and repeat the process.

then kicked out toward the rising fish. I let the fly drag out of the way, 20 feet behind the tube. Bam! I had a fish on before I'd traveled 50 feet. While playing and landing the 17-inch rainbow, I noticed several other fish taking caddis off the surface. Man, was I excited!

I worked my way out to where most of the fish were rising, then cast and let the fly sit motionless, anxiously awaiting another take. Nothing happened. I picked up and cast to other rising trout. Again, nothing! It wasn't until I decided to move position and drag my fly along the surface that I picked up another fish.

Suddenly it clicked: the trout were taking the caddis as they scooted across the surface. These caddis were a species known as "traveling sedge," an insect that runs across the water, and that is when the trout take them: while they are running.

After that recognition, I skated caddis imitations across the surface of Chopaka Lake until darkness drove me from the water. I can't even guess how many fish I caught and released that evening.

The next morning I awoke to a howling snowstorm, and remembering the hill I'd traveled to get to camp, I packed up in a hurry and headed out.

I have returned to Chopaka a number of times in spring and fall and have always found good fishing. Other anglers have complained of being shut out on this lake, particularly in summer, but spring and fall have always been productive for me.

I concentrate my efforts at the edges of the lake, along the tules and in the weedbeds. When things do get slow, I have been told that trolling a wet fly or streamer along the deeper northern shore can be effective.

Ranch Lakes, late October

The trout in the photographs were of monstrous proportions. Until I was invited to the Isaac Ranch Lakes to do a story for a national fishing magazine, I had only dreamed of trout that size. In fact, I don't think I really expected I would ever catch one so humongous.

It was a calm, chilly fall morning when I met the guide at a little cafe near Coulee City in central Washington. It was another 45 minutes or so to the lakes. Along the way, my thoughts were filled with visions of trophy trout.

George Cook, a sales representative for Sage rods, is responsible for the fishing at Isaac Ranch. The lakes are located in natural depressions in the rolling hills of this arid farmland. Ranch Lakes, as they are commonly known, were originally created for irrigation purposes. Then George worked out a deal with the land owners. The lakes were enlarged, aerated, and eventually stocked with a

Washington's Private Fisheries

RANCH LAKES (Douglas Co.)
Contact: 360-779-3769
Price: $162.50/rod/day
Species: Rainbow and brown to 10 lbs.
Season: Ice-off to June, then Sept. to ice-up

WALKER LAKE FISHING CAMP (Okanogan Co.)
Contact: 509-486-1270
Price: $120/rod/day (includes lodging)
Species: Rainbow, brown, Kamloops 12-30 inches
Specifics: 45 acres, spring fed; main lodge, ten bedrooms
Season- May through Oct.

DREAM LAKE: (Snohomish Co.)
Contact 360-568-1978
Price: $95/rod/day
Species: Rainbow, Kamloops, average 5 -8 lbs.
Specifics: 5 acres
Season: October through May

SORENSON LAKE: (Kittitas Co.)
Contact: Evening Hatch Guide Service 509-574-8334
Price: $100/rod/half-day, $135/rod/full day
Species: Rainbow to 6 lbs.
Specifics: 14 acres
Season: ice-off to mid-June, then mid-Sept. to ice-up

carefully selected number of trout. With the abundant food supply and little competition, the trout grew big in a hurry.

The plan was to manage the lakes with just enough fish to grow to trophy proportions. Catch-and-release fly fishing would be the

Ranch Lakes are stocked with just enough fish to maintain a trophy fishery.

rule, since this method of fishing is generally less harmful to the fish than any other. A rod fee was established, and fly anglers were soon booking openings.

When I pulled into the parking area by the main lake, I remember thinking, *Trophy trout come outta here?* Surrounded by grass and sage covered hills, the lake seemed small. The unpleasant hum I heard when I got out of my car turned out to be a high-voltage powerline that crossed the lake. I wasn't impressed.

Then suddenly, out of the corner of my eye, I saw a fish break the surface—a large fish. The rings were as big as if a man had fallen in. I donned my waders and assembled my rod with shaking hands.

Although I'd brought a float tube, the guide told me tubes are seldom needed to reach the fish. There are no real obstacles to hinder a backcast, so putting a fly in front of a fish cruising offshore is not a problem for anyone with moderate casting ability.

We waded in up to our knees and cast black leech patterns as far as we could. Strip, pause. Strip, pause. Before I could strip my line all the way back in, I had a fish on, but it didn't feel like the desert trout I was used to. Instead of fast, short head-shaking bouts, this fish authoritatively tore line off in long runs, thrashing about like a salmon.

When the big rainbow finally came into view, I understood the difference. A couple of heart-stopping grabs and misses later, I brought the tired fish to my feet and shakily released my first eight-pound trout from Upper Ranch lake.

Throughout the day we caught several trout in the same size range. It was absolutely the best fishing I had ever had. Subsequent trips have been equally thrilling.

Since my first trip, George has introduced trout (both rainbow and browns) into Lower Ranch lake. These fish have done exceptionally well. A few years ago George sent me photos of fish taken from this lake, a rainbow and a brown, each over ten pounds!

Ranch Lakes contain the same types of aquatic foods found in any desert lake: chironomids in spring, then damsels, dragons, and a few mayflies. Scuds and leeches can be effective throughout the open season.

"Pay" fisheries are not for everyone, and I certainly don't fish them often myself. But if you'd like to catch a truly trophy trout (and a trip to Alaska or some other expensive, exotic, big-trout destination is out of the question), a pay-to-play fishery like Ranch Lakes is a fair substitute.

There are more pay fisheries opening up all the time, including one in the Ellensburg area and another on Walker Lake, near Tonasket in north-central Washington. Another pay lake may be opening near Ranch Lakes. Most of these pay lakes book through fly shops, so check with your local fly shop for information.

Bass, Bass, and More Bass

Deep River, early October

The day was bright—too bright for searun cutthroat, which was what my boys and I had set out to catch. After a couple of futile hours tromping the banks of one of our favorite coastal streams, Luke and Jordan convinced me we should bag the fishing, get some candy, and go home.

Driving towards Raymond along State Highway 4, we crossed Deep River about two miles above its confluence with the Columbia at Gray's Bay. From the bridge, I noticed a lily pad covered slough off to the left and remembered a magazine article I'd read about bass fishing in southwest Washington. The author said bass and panfish could be found in nearly every slough and pond in this corner of the state, especially in those associated with the Columbia River.

A couple miles past the bridge, I pulled the car over, did a quick U-turn, and headed back to the slough. The kids had their tackle boxes with them, and I knew each had at least enough grubs and spinnerbaits to see if there were any fish at home.

Early fall often brings rain showers and sun breaks within minutes of one another. After parking the car below Deep River Bridge, we waited out the approaching squall. The rain came on fast, ended quickly, and within minutes the sun was again baking the heavy, west-side vegetation. A rich, humid, earthy smell rose out of the grass as we made our way toward the water.

The faint trail we followed ran along a dike. Blackberry runners reached out aggressively, snagging and tripping us, and soaking our pant legs. Eventually we came to a little opening from which we could see a couple of culverts that ran under the dike, connecting the slough to a slow, tidewater section of Deep River. The tide was running in, creating a bit of current through the culvert. This looked like the perfect spot to begin exploring.

The boys each tied a small spinnerbait with curly-tailed grub to their lines and cast into a narrow channel created by the tidal flow among the lily pads. Their very first retrieves produced a small bass for each. Not a bad start!

We spent a couple of hours in that one spot. Between them, the boys landed two-dozen bass and a half-dozen black crappie.

Later, while driving home, my mind raced with the possibilities. There are countless sloughs along the highways of southwest Washington, not to mention several little lakes which were mentioned in the article I'd read. I vowed (not for the first time!) to devote more time to exploring southwest Washington's bass water.

Over the years I have followed up on my intention, often going out on autumn evenings for an hour or so, taking along a fly rod and handful of poppers. A good number of the waters I've explored were productive, and all had some features in common. They were shallow, and thick with weeds or lily pads. Shallow meant that top-water baits (my favorite) could be used effectively. Weedy meant that Texas-style worm rigs and other weedless baits were a must. These waters also had an additional feature in common—there were no other anglers!

Among the better bass waters I have explored in this part of the state are O'Neil Lake (a 10-acre lake inside Fort Canby State Park, just south of Ilwaco) and several lakes on the Long Beach Peninsula north of Long Beach (Clam Lake, Clear Lake, Cranberry Lake, and Island Lake). And there are many more in which I have yet to wet a line, including the numerous sloughs along the Columbia.

The longer I fish Washington, the more I am amazed at how much there is still to discover. The more crowded the hot spots and glamour fisheries get, the more I am drawn to Washington's unexplored warm water fisheries.

Spring Creek Trout

Rocky Ford Creek, mid-October

Pinky Freeman's old truck fishtailed a bit as we rattled over the washboarded road. A passing car stirred up the dust so thick we decided to stop a few minutes and let the air clear. The barbed wire fence that lined the gravel road was plugged with tumbleweed, testimony to the wind that often howls through the eastern Washington desert. We had turned off Highway 17 a few miles southwest of Ephrata. After two rough miles, we arrived at our destination—Rocky Ford Spring Creek—at a point very near its source.

A fly-fishing-only trout stream, Rocky Ford is renowned for its difficulty. I had heard stories of this oasis in the desert, and of its large, hard-to-catch rainbows. While fishing at nearby Lake Lenore on this warm fall afternoon, Pinky and I decided the time had come to check the stories out for ourselves. After all, it couldn't be that difficult! Or could it?

We pulled into the WDFW parking lot near the bottom of the hill, and as we strung our three-weight rods with floating line (all that's needed here), we noticed anglers scattered along the creek as far as we could see. Having fished some of Montana's famous spring creeks, this didn't bother me much. I knew that spring creek trout are used to seeing people and aren't easily spooked by a human silhouette. However, spring creek trout are also used to seeing phony insects, and they feed cautiously because of that. Hence their reputation for being difficult.

After lengthening our leaders to 16 feet, with the last five feet a limp tippet tapered to 6X, we made our way towards the creek. Observing the other anglers as we approached, we couldn't help but notice a lot of casting—and no bent rods.

Sneaking up to the waters edge, our mouths dropped open. Trout—large trout—could be seen feeding in every direction, the white insides of their mouths clearly visible in stark contrast with the surreal green of the aquatic vegetation. They were feeding on something very small and near the bottom, but we couldn't tell what. No adult insects were in the air, save for a few tiny midges. We backed off and shakily dug out our boxes of minute flies.

Seeing large trout feeding always gets my adrenaline pumping, which is not the best of conditions for handling minuscule flies. After regaining a bit of control, Pinky and I each selected small nymphs from our boxes. He chose a small Hare's Ear; I opted for a micro-midge, both reasonable selections under the circumstances.

We crept back to the water and each picked out a cruising, feeding rainbow. Delicately, our flies touched down. With anticipation building, our trembling hands were ready to strike. But nothing happened. Our flies were ignored.

We each picked up and cast again to different fish. "Here comes one," I whispered to myself. "Here comes. Here comes. Damn!" Ignored again!

Obviously, we were using the wrong flies. So we changed. And we changed again. And we changed some more. And we changed until we didn't have any new flies to change to.

A guy came walking down the trail. He stopped beside Pinky and me and asked how the fishing was. He was obviously new to fly angling—it was written all over his aura, attire, and gear.

He was nearly ecstatic when he saw all the big fish swimming around. We couldn't help but sneak peeks as he fumbled around in his fly box, which appeared to contain upwards of a dozen large, poorly proportioned flies. He selected a huge Mickey Finn streamer, a size 4, and tied it to his hefty leader, which appeared not to taper at all. Pinky and I gave each other one of those, *this guy hasn't got a chance* grins, and went back to our growing frustration.

The splashdown when his heavy line and monstrous fly landed on the surface of the creek echoed up and down the bank. So did his whoop and holler when a sizeable trout bent his rod double.

Pinky looked at me, and in a stoic voice said, "Sometimes tech-

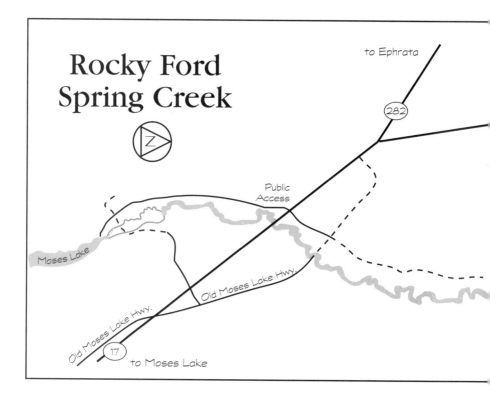

Rocky Ford
Spring Creek

to Ephrata

282

Public
Access

Moses Lake

Old Moses Lake Hwy.

Old Moses Lake Hwy.

17

to Moses Lake

nical fly fishing just don't figure!" We packed up our gear and left, humbled and grim.

Most of the time, Rocky Ford Spring Creek *is* a technical fishery—which means successful anglers need a good understanding of entomology, presentation, and technique.

Since the water in spring creeks bubbles up from the ground, water temperature remains fairly constant for the first few miles. A constant temperature means that anglers can count on the presence of the same aquatic insects year 'round, and on reliable hatches. At Rocky Ford, as in most spring creeks, insect hatches often overlap or come in multiples. And more often than not, the bugs are small.

Rocky Ford Spring Creek rambles roughly six miles from its source before emptying into Moses Lake. Public access to the upper

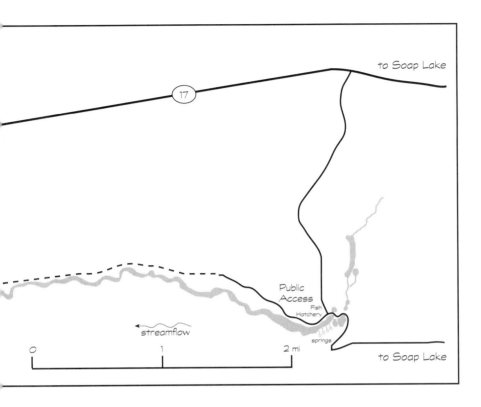

creek is from a gravel road off Highway 17. There is also a parking area with access a few miles south of this point, where the creek travels under Highway 17. This lower section of Rocky Ford is wide and slow.

Trout hatcheries have long played a role in this rich fishery. In the late 1980s, a privately-owned hatchery was built on state land at the head of the creek at the site of an abandoned hatchery. By agreement with the state, the hatchery provides fish for stocking in other waters and carries out habitat improvement projects on Rocky Ford. When the hatchery was built, the creek was rehabilitated to remove carp, then trout of all sizes were stocked.

When my friend John Worrall came to visit from Wyoming one autumn, we met Michael and Christine Fong over at Dry Falls Lake, planning to spend the day there. But the water temperature was

Rocky Ford Tips

Since Rocky Ford's current is slow, the trout have plenty of time to scrutinize the food they eat, and they see plenty of fake bugs. Consequently, it is generally imperative to exactly match the size and color of the natural foods. Midges, mayflies, caddisflies, scuds, dragonfly nymphs, damselfly nymphs, leeches and back swimmers are all present in large numbers and in various stages of their life cycles.

Leaders need to be long, 12 to 16 feet with long tippets of 5X or 6X . The lighter the tippet, the better your odds for a hook-up. On the other hand, when a large fish takes you into the weeds, the odds of landing that fish are greatly reduced on light tippet.

My selection of fly patterns for Rocky Ford includes Griffith's Gnat (size 18), Baetis Parachute (size 18), Adams Parachute (sizes 18 and 20), Gray Midge Pupa (size 20), Brassie (size 20), Olive Scud (sizes 16-20), and TDC Chironomid Pupa (sizes 16 and 18).

unseasonably warm, so we headed for Rocky Ford, my ace-in-the-hole for visiting anglers.

There was an exceptional amount of drifting vegetation on the water, a problem more often encountered during the hot summer months. Presentation was difficult, and as usual, so were the trout. Michael and I each eventually took a few nice rainbows, but that's not the point of this story. My friend John is the focus here.

Walking along the stream, John and I were engaged in the usual fishermen's babble when John asked, "Any snakes around here?" Just as he asked the question, I spotted a small rattlesnake in the path, no more than five feet ahead of us. I grabbed his arm, stopping him, and said casually, "Sure, lots of snakes. See, you almost stepped on that one!"Some people are afraid of snakes, and some people are *afraid* of snakes!

There are rattlesnakes around Rocky Ford Spring Creek, but

Rocky Ford is known for its large, hard-to-catch rainbows.

with a little caution, and some common sense, they shouldn't pose a problem.

Rocky Ford is open to public fishing along two sections managed by WDFW. One is along the upper one mile of the creek, and the other is on the lower three miles. Although this isn't a lot of stream, the number and size of trout packed into those stretches definitely makes a visit worthwhile. Wading is not allowed in Rocky Ford, but since much of the stream is swampy at the edges, you will need some sort of waterproof shoe or low boot if you want to keep your feet dry.

Washington's famous spring creek is a worthy destination in its own right, but if you're fishing the nearby lakes, you really ought to stop by Rocky Ford and give it a shot. Though frustrating and demanding, spring creeks help us hone our angling skills . . . and keep us humble.

Coastal River Salmon

October

It was hard to see the river through the fog in the half-light of dawn. The morning was damp and chill, but somewhere in the distance, probably in the lower part of the pool, a salmon splashed, then another. It was what I'd been hoping for. The previous day we'd had a good rain, just enough to bring the first salmon in from the salt.

I knotted a big Flash-Glo spinner to my line and began casting into the haze. After an hour of mindless effort, I was beginning to think that maybe I should have stayed home in bed. Then, out of the blue, my size 5 spinner was intercepted by a 30-pound, fresh-from-the-salt chinook salmon.

Battling a big salmon in tight quarters is something you have to experience in order to understand. A sense of urgency mingles with one of impending doom. I landed the fish, but that's not always the case, not by a long shot.

Salmon in fresh water are never a sure thing. Even if fish are jumping all over the place, making contact with one of them is not a certainty. The factors that make the difference are subject to endless debate.

For sure, salmon need enough water to encourage them to travel upstream. Many people have the impression that it rains all the time at the Washington coast. In reality, summer and early fall can be dry as a bone. During long periods without rain, salmon will stack up in tidewater and wait for a freshet before heading up river. Meanwhile, salmon anglers cool their heels, hoping for rain.

When the rain finally does come, it often comes in a big way, falling incessantly for a few days, knocking the rivers out of shape. While the stream remains unfit to fish (high and brown), salmon shoot upstream.

The best scenario for salmon fishing is a few gentle rains scattered throughout the fall, bringing the salmon in at a steady, moderate rate. This actually happens occasionally. And when it does, I am on the stream nearly every day.

Willapa River, early October

The Willapa River flows through the small town of Raymond in southwest Washington, where I have lived for the past 20 years. It was on the Willapa that I caught my first river salmon. I was actually fly fishing for cutthroat on the upper  Willapa when it happened, and the incident took me so much by surprise that I will never forget it.

As I was walking along the river, working over the pools, a large swirl appeared beside my Skykomish Sunrise just as it touched down. I was shaken. Surely that must have been the largest searun cutthroat in the entire river. I picked up and cast again. The moment my fly hit the water, it disappeared into the mouth of a large chinook salmon that, I later discovered, uncharacteristically came to the surface to take it.

As you can imagine, my adrenaline was on full throttle as I played the big salmon, and I wasn't always in control of the moment. Sometime during the battle, the fly line wrapped around the tip of my vintage bamboo fly rod, and during one period of aggressive thrashing, about six inches of rod tip snapped like a toothpick. I managed to land and release the brute, and my excitement was such that I didn't even mourn my broken rod until much later.

Needless to say, I don't fly fish for salmon with a bamboo rod anymore. In fact, when the fish are well into the river system, pursuing them with a fly is probably the least productive method you can use. The most effective way to take salmon in fresh water is with egg clusters, sandshrimp, or other natural bait.

When fishing egg clusters or sandshrimp, most anglers use the typical steelhead or salmon outfit: a spinning or casting rod, and a reel loaded with 10- to 15-pound monofilament line. A size 2 egg-loop hook is preferred, often with a twist of yarn, a Corkie, or both. The offering is then bounced along the bottom through pools, below riffles, or in any area slow and deep enough for salmon to hold.

It takes some practice to recognize the feel of a salmon take. Though you might expect something more dramatic, a salmon picking up your bait often feels like nothing more than a pecking trout. My rule of thumb is to set the hook at any variation in the drift. Be prepared to be surprised by the weight of a fresh salmon.

Shortly after moving to the coast, my wife, Cindy, and I went out one afternoon to try our luck on the Willapa. We had heard fresh salmon were being caught, so armed with spinning rods and fresh roe, we headed for the river. We drove the short distance along Highway 6 east of town until we came to an area known at that time as the Chip Hole. This is the first good salmon pool above tidewater.

When "silvers" and "dogs" are running in the Satsop, word travels fast.

It takes practice to recognize the peck of a salmon. (Willapa River coho)

Flies (clockwise from top): Halfarabbit, Hair Popper, Mylar Baitfish, Gray Hackle Yellow, Goddard Caddis, V-Rib Chironomid, Night Leech, Saltwater Baitfish.

Puget Sound's many feeder streams provide good habitat for sea-run.

The Willapa is open to boat fishing below Camp One Bridge.

Cindy began casting into the slower water while I fished a slot just below the riffle. Immediately I hooked, landed, and released a chinook jack (an immature salmon). Then Cindy let out a holler and began battle with what was apparently a much larger fish—the first salmon she had ever connected with on a river.

The fish raced around the pool once or twice, then her line went slack.

"Dang! I lost it! And now I'm snagged on the bottom."

I made another cast and caught another jack from the same water where I'd taken the other.

"Will you come get me free?" she pleaded.

Walking over to her, I noticed that she had given up trying to break free of the snag. She was sitting on a rock, rod lying in the mud beside her. I picked up the rod and reeled in the slack. When I gave a sharp pull, I felt a tug on the other end. Another sharp pull and . . .

The battle lasted twenty minutes. When all was said and done, Cindy posed with a 25-pound fall chinook. She also learned just

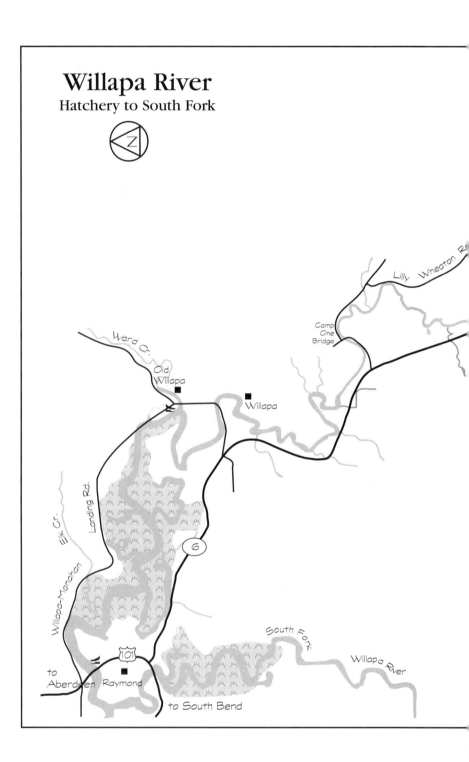

Willapa River
Hatchery to South Fork

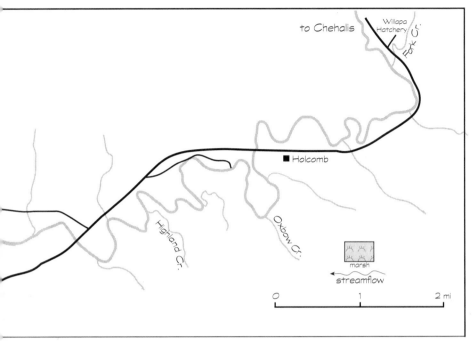

how fast and strong a chinook salmon in a river can be. From then on, whenever she "snagged up," she always gave the rod an extra strong jerk—just to make sure!

One of the biggest problems with fishing the Willapa is access. Most of the river runs through private farmland, but there are several access points along Highway 6, which parallels the Willapa throughout much of its fishable length. The best way to identify these access points is to drive until you spot cars parked along the highway. When the salmon are in, the fishing folks will be out! Where you find parked cars, you will usually find a trail leading to the water.

There are two public boat ramps on the lower Willapa. One is right in the town of Raymond, the other a few miles to the east in the small community know as Old Willapa. Fishing from boats is not allowed upstream of the Camp One Bridge, but trollers do very well in the tidewater sections downstream of the bridge. Most people slow-troll a big Flash-Glo or similar spinner. When fresh fish are thick, slow-trolling is one of the best ways to take them.

Chinook salmon are the first to enter Washington's coastal rivers in the fall, coming with the September rains. These large salmon are followed and overlapped by the smaller and more aggressive coho salmon. In general, you can use the same gear for the coho, though most coho anglers prefer spinners and spoons to bait. More coho than chinook enter the Willapa, and the coho catch is significantly greater.

Like several other coastal rivers, the Willapa also gets a second run of late season coho that enter throughout late fall and winter. The few extra months in the ocean add pounds to these late arrivals, and it isn't uncommon to take coho from 15 to 20 pounds from November through January. I usually target a few of these late season coho for my smokehouse just before Christmas.

Satsop River, early November

When salmon are running in the rivers of western Washington, word travels fast. One fall evening, Pinky Freeman called with a report that silvers (coho salmon) and dogs (chum salmon) were running in the Satsop, which is about a 45-minute drive from Raymond. The crisp air of pre-dawn found us standing with several other anglers at the edge of the Satsop River waiting for enough light to cast.

As we waited, we heard the whooping and hollering of someone downstream who was obviously already into a fish. Without another word, we all plunged in, and a barrage of casts splashed down on the far side of the pool.

Literally within seconds there were more "fish on" sounds, and within minutes, Pinky was into a fish. Through the gray light, I could make out at least four rods bent under the weight of salmon.

Pinky and I generally fly fish the Satsop, using nine-weight rods with egg fly patterns cast to the far bank. We've landed many chinook, coho, and chum with these rigs, though not nearly as many as do bait anglers. Still, when we do tie into one, it's an experience to savor all winter.

There are only a few public access points along the Satsop River. A boat ramp just off Highway 12 near the town of Satsop offers access to the lower river and to the Chehalis, which the Satsop joins within a couple of miles. If you follow the East Satsop Road out of town, you can make contact with the river in a few places between the town and Schafer State Park. When the fish are in, you can't miss the access points; just watch for vehicles packed into any and every wide spot in the road within walking distance of the water.

Hoh River, early November

Just after crossing the Hoh River, Highway 101 veers left and climbs a steep hill. Pay attention, and you'll see a road to the right that leads down to the river and to Oxbow Campground. On this trip, I overshot my turn in the dark and  had to backtrack. When I arrived, a couple driftboats were waiting in line as another was preparing to launch.

My plan was to bank fish a few hours for chinook before meeting a guide in Forks, then we'd drift the upper river for steelhead. I only had a couple of hours before my rendezvous.

By the time I was done fiddling with my gear, all the boats had launched. On my way down to the river, I saw another bank angler preparing his tackle.

I decided to talk with the fellow and see if he had been fishing lately. He looked a bit defensive as I approached, but mellowed when we started talking.

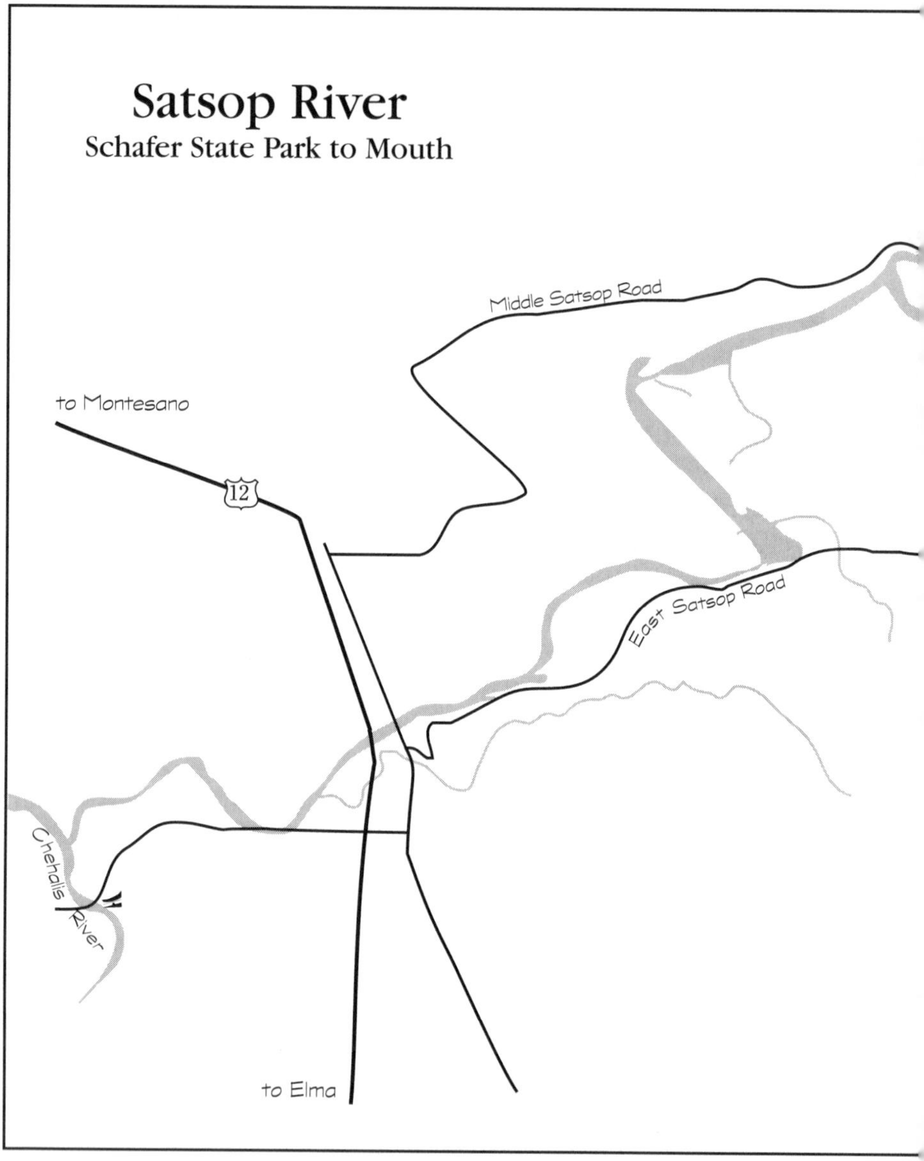

Satsop River
Schafer State Park to Mouth

Middle Satsop Road

to Montesano

12

East Satsop Road

Chehalis River

to Elma

"Been fishin'?" I asked.

"Yesterday, and the day before," he replied. "Caught three big kings right here in this hole."

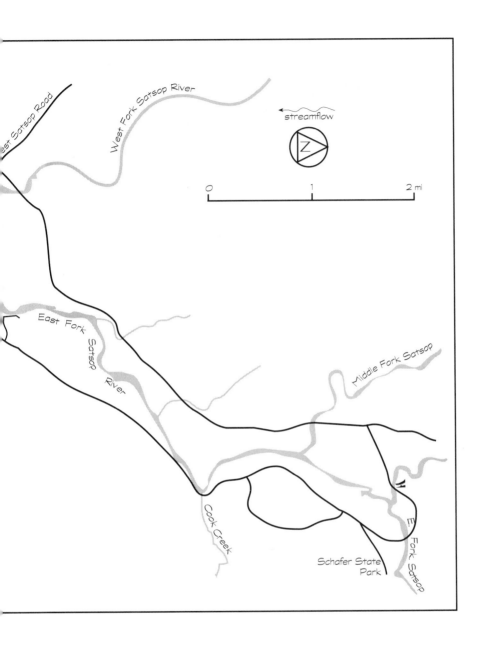

We talked fishing until he finished rigging his rod with a side planer and plug. A side planer is a device that allows a bank angler to work a plug back and forth in the same manner as from a boat. I

Most coastal rivers host overlapping runs of chinook, coho, and steelhead.

moved upstream a ways to try my luck. Using a spinning rod, I knotted a large hammered brass spoon to my 15-pound line and began casting into the silty, glacial waters of the Hoh.

The stretch of river at the Oxbow Camp is long, broad, and slow—ideal holding water for salmon. There is enough bank access to accommodate several anglers here. Surprisingly, there were only two of us fishing it that morning.

Within fifteen minutes I heard a commotion downstream. The plug fisherman had one on, and from the bend in his rod, it appeared to be a significant fish. I snagged up, broke off, and ran down to take pictures of the battle, but before I could get there, the fish broke free. The guy started cursing and stomping around, so I did a 180 and headed back to my rod.

I could have re-rigged and fished a few minutes more, but at that point, if I hooked a salmon and had the opportunity to play it, I'd be late for my steelheading rendezvous in Forks.

As it turned out, our steelhead trip was uneventful, though we did see a couple of other anglers land big chinook during the float.

Like most rivers on the Washington coast, the Hoh has overlapping runs of chinook, coho, and steelhead. The best way to fish it is from a driftboat, and there are a half-dozen possible launch sites, including a couple on the lower river off Highway 101.

The Hoh is a big river, and most anglers use medium to heavy gear when fishing it for salmon—a baitcasting or spinning rod with a large capacity reel loaded with monofilament line ranging from 10- to 20-pound breaking strength.

Water condition is the most important consideration when fishing here. It rains a lot on the Olympic Peninsula, and the temperate rain forest through which the Hoh flows receives well over 100 inches of precipitation each year. A healthy rain or warm temperatures will discolor this glacial river in a hurry. Before making a trip to the Hoh, it is always best to call for river conditions (Olympic Sporting Goods, Forks, 360-374-6330).

To drift the Hoh, you should have at least intermediate rowing skills. Though you will seldom encounter extreme technical problems on the river, frequent floods (several each year) produce logjams and other hazards, so beware!

Sea-run Cutthroat

South Puget Sound, late-October

I don't know if we could have cut it with a knife, but the fog was so thick we couldn't see 30 feet in front of our boat. The water was eerily flat for tidewater. The only disturbance was the occasional ring left by a sea bird feeding on the surface and the churn of our outboard motor as we chugged along on a slow troll.

We followed the irregular shoreline, keeping the little aluminum boat about 40 feet from shore in water just deep enough that we could barely make out the rock and shell covered bottom. We were trolling small, four-inch herring on trout rods. My fishing partners were my dad and Buz Reynolds, a friend who lives along a sheltered bay of Puget Sound near the little community of Purdy. This day was to be my introduction to sea-run cutthroat trout.

It was late fall, the ideal time to be searching for cutthroat here, according to Buz. He'd spent his childhood fishing these waters, mostly trolling the shorelines near the family home. I was mesmerized by the rhythmic chug-chug of the outboard, my rod tip slightly twitching as the herring danced 50 feet behind the boat. My eyes grew heavy and my head was bobbing when the line tightened and throbbed under the weight of a sea-run, a fat 16-incher. As with all firsts, the image of my first sea-run remains crystal clear—its dark olive back with a scar behind the dorsal fin, heavily spotted sides, sea lice clinging to its back, and that distinctive orange slash under the jaw.

Fishing with Buz and my dad became an annual ritual. We fished several areas around this part of Puget Sound and nearly al-

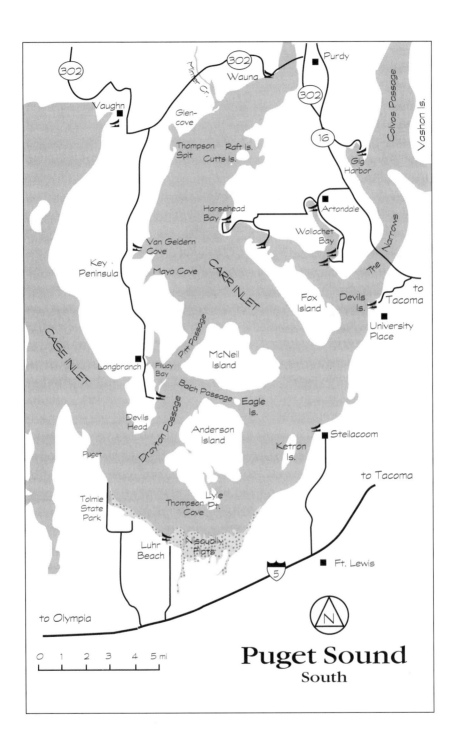

Puget Sound
South

ways found sea-runs. I began experimenting with other types of tackle and found that spinners, spoons, plugs, and even flies worked well. Sea-run cutthroat quickly became my favorite quarry. They were the first "saltwater" fish I ever caught, adding greatly to the excitement of my early fishing years.

Today, sea-run are still special to me. Not only do they remind me of my youth and of those early outings with my dad, but they also evoke all the feelings that I have for Washington's native fish. As I walk in solitude along the little streams of western Washington these days in search of the elusive cutthroat, I feel a great sense of peace, enjoying the quiet autumn walk even if I don't find fish.

Sea-run cutthroat on the Washington coast have had their ups and downs, but the Puget Sound fishery has always been produc-tive. The Sound's many feeder streams provide good spawning habitat, while the biologically rich waters of the Sound offer ideal feeding grounds, growing some of the largest cutthroat in the state. In fact, the state record sea-run comes from Puget Sound's Carr Inlet. Caught back in 1943, it weighed in at six pounds.

When sea-run cutthroat return to the sea in early spring, they seldom wander far from their home inlets. Unlike steelhead and salmon, they prefer the estuaries and inshore waters like the Sound, generally traveling in small schools, following the tide, feeding on shrimp, baitfish, and other tasty morsels along the shoreline.

Any bay, cove, or stream flowing into the Sound might host sea-run. Looking at a map of the Sound, you can see that the fishing opportunities are almost staggering. To narrow your choices, pay particular attention to rocky shorelines, oyster beds, and stream mouths—all of which tend to concentrate the food sources that attract sea-run. Sheltered bays and gravel beaches are also good sea-run locators.

You almost have to have a boat to fish the Sound, though small cartop boats are all that's needed when fishing the sheltered shorelines. Access is generally good, with boat ramps well marked both on the roads and on highway maps.

Hood Canal offers additional inland sea-run opportunities, similar to those of the Sound.

South Fork Willapa River, mid-October

Historically, nearly every stream in western Washington that drains into the ocean once hosted sea-run cutthroat. In recent years, some of these runs have fallen victim to overharvest, pollution, and careless logging practices. Fortunately, the cutthroat are making a comeback in many Washington streams, thanks to thoughtful management and conservation programs, and to the cooperation and assistance of citizen volunteers and angling organizations.

Shortly after moving to the little coastal town of Raymond, I overheard a couple of old timers in a local sporting goods store talking about the good cutthroat fishing they'd been having on the South Fork of the Willapa River, just outside of town. It had been a long fishless spell for me, so by first light the next morning I was at the river, fly rod in hand.

I walked along the small stream, casting in all the places that seemed likely to hold a trout—the same places I'd cast for trout in eastern Washington where I grew up. I hit the riffles, tailouts, flats, etc. But I drew a blank. Not one fish. Where were all of those cutthroat that I heard about while eavesdropping?

The next morning I hit the stream again. While trying to cast a fly into a narrow slot below a riffle, I overshot the target, sending my offering into the slack, leaf-covered, stagnant water on the other side. I quickly began stripping line to get the fly into the slot, but to my surprise, there was a flash and a heavy tug as a sizeable fish twisted and turned at the end of the line. After an intense battle, I admired, photographed, and released my first river-caught sea-run cutthroat, a beautifully colored, heavily spotted fish about 14-inches long.

Wondering why that cutthroat was in the slack water, I nevertheless cast my fly back into the same slow water—and caught another fish. At that point, I stopped asking questions and just concentrated my casts in the "frog water"—the foam-covered stagnant water that I would normally avoid when trout fishing. And I caught fish. By the end of the day, I was staggering with excitement.

I spent the rest of that fall exploring streams near my new home, in search of sea-run. I found that nearly all the streams contained sea-run cutthroat, and that these fish were not fussy eaters. Though they would attack almost any sunken lure or fly I tossed their way, the most effective flies were heavily hackled wets such as the Gray Hackle Yellow and Skykomish Sunrise, in size 6. Among the spinners, a small Mepps or small Roostertail were hard to beat.

Sea-run cutthroat are found in streams from Prince William Sound in southern Alaska to the Eel River in California. They range inland as far as Washington's Cascade crest. Sea-runs enter their spawning stream from mid-summer through winter (depending on their range), and spawn in early spring in little headwaters and tributary streams. In Washington, peak sea-run returns are in September or October, hence their nickname, "harvest trout."

Searun are often found in the slack water trout anglers avoid.

Not all sea-runs that return to freshwater are capable of spawning. In fact, studies show that as many as half the returning fish are sexually immature. But of those mature fish that do return, up to 40 percent may survive to spawn again, with considerably fewer fish returning to spawn for a third or fourth time.

In the coastal streams of southwest Washington, sea-run cutthroat generally run 10 to 14 inches long, with some 18 inches or more. A cutthroat over 15 inches is considered a prize. It is interesting to note that streams in the same general area, even draining into the same estuary, may characteristically host sea-run trout of different average sizes. For example, the Naselle River, a good cutthroat stream that drains into Willapa Bay, hosts larger fish than does the Nemah River, which also drains into Willapa.

Like every other anadramous species in the Northwest, sea-run cutthroat have fallen victim to "progress." Their worst enemy has probably been careless logging practices in coastal headwaters where the cutthroat spawn. Clearcuts can completely destroy the ability of small feeder streams to support fish. Unstable flows and excessive warming of the water are a big problem. Fry also become easy targets for predators without the cover of protective vegetation.

Over-harvest has also been an issue. Those same "old timers" who have shared cutthroat stories with me tell of the "good old days" when you could fill a gunnysack full of cutthroat from any number of streams. Fortunately, bag limits today are more conservation minded, with a two-fish daily bag limit and 14-inch minimum size in most waters.

Hatchery-reared cutthroat have been planted in a number of Western Washington streams, particularly those that have suffered most severely from overharvest, poor logging practices, and other abuses. All hatchery fish have a clipped adipose fin. Many (though not all) Washington streams require the release of wild cutthroat trout (those without a clipped adipose fin). Before fishing a western Washington stream, read the WDFW *Sport Fishing Rules* for that water.

With any luck, in years to come, when the first fall freshets arrive and the vine maples turn crimson—there will be sea-run cutthroat for our children to fish.

Winter

In Washington, summer slips gradually into fall. Some years, the two seasons almost blend into one gloriously long fishing bonanza. Winter, on the other hand, always sneaks up on me, catching me off guard. Maybe it's because I live on the west side of the mountains, where the passing of fall into winter only means that the rain gets colder. In blissful ignorance, I'll drive to one of my favorite eastside lakes and be startled when it begins to snow!

For some people, northwest winters are depressing, but most of them aren't anglers. If you're into fishing in a big way like I am, winter rain doesn't just mean cold and wet—it means steelhead! When westside rivers rise to their winter levels and the temperatures drop, steelhead won't be far behind.

Steelhead are the primary focus of my winter fishing, but there are other opportunities available for anglers who refuse to let winter shut them down. Many Washington trout and bass lakes are open year 'round, and during exceptionally cold winters there are opportunities to ice fish the lakes of eastern Washington. Resident salmon are available in Puget Sound. And whitefish come into their own as a targeted sport fish once trout season ends on Washington's streams.

Winter Steelhead

Queets River, late November

The driving rain was not a good sign. I wondered why I'd left my snug bed to drive three hours to a river that almost certainly would be out of shape. But by the time Tim Mondale and I reached the road to Queets River Campground, the rain had all but stopped. Thirteen rough miles later, the sun was making an effort to punch through the clouds.

Even if the river was high and muddy, the trip would have been worth it. The road passed through the lush Queets Rainforest of Olympic National Park, one of few temperate rainforests in the world. Towering fir and cedar trees line the way, their moss-laden branches forming an emerald canopy over the road. We saw two herds of Roosevelt elk, and grinned like kids looking at the world through colored cellophane when occasional bursts of sun bathed us in a surreal green glow.

When we reached the campground, it was deserted. Every time I show up at a fishing hole and nobody's there, I get a feeling that everyone else knows something I don't. Maybe there was a sudden closure on the river, or a wild man-eating grizzly was loose in the campground, or even something more simple—like the nearest fish was 100 miles away!

But the truth was, everyone else had the same gut feeling I'd had when I woke up: *surely the river's been blown out of shape.* But it wasn't. It was as perfect as perfect gets on a glacier-fed river. And we had it all to ourselves.

The water was deep green, a sure sign that the freezing level was not far above us, and little or no glacial melt was taking place. If the air temperature had been higher, the water would have been a

The author with a Queets River steelhead.

dirty-aqua color. The flow was just right, too, and as we slipped our Tote 'N Floats (personal kick boats) into the icy water, I felt a rush of adrenaline and was glad I hadn't slept in.

Immediately downstream from the put-in, we maneuvered our little boats through Sams Rapids, one of two rapids in the boatable stretch from the campground to the park boundary (the boating deadline). Beyond the boundary, the river flows through the Quinault Reservation and is off-limits for non-tribal members.

Before you get any bright ideas about floating this river (or any other river for that matter) in a personal kick-boat, I must tell you that the boats we were using had modified oarlock systems and six and a half-foot oars. Although the rapids on this river are short on white water, there is an abundance of rocks and log jams that need to be maneuvered around, so you need a maneuverable, river-worthy craft and some experience.

After rowing through the rock garden of Sams Rapids, we pulled our little boats to shore and began fishing the slick below. My partner was using a jig and float; I opted for fly tackle. We worked

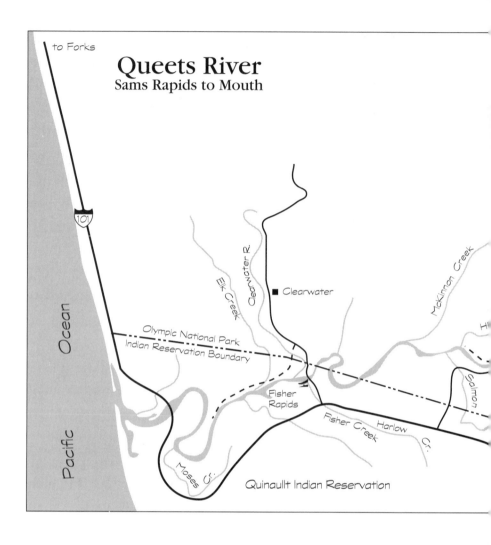

Queets River
Sams Rapids to Mouth

our way downstream, thoroughly covering the best steelhead water we could find—the drifts below riffles, along banks, and around rocks. I changed flies regularly; my buddy kept on with the jig and float. Both of us drew blanks.

About halfway through our six-mile float, while fishing a slow, deep bend, Tim hooked into a big, bright steelhead that immediately launched into an acrobatic show that took my breath away. There is little in the fishing world that excites me more than a big, wild

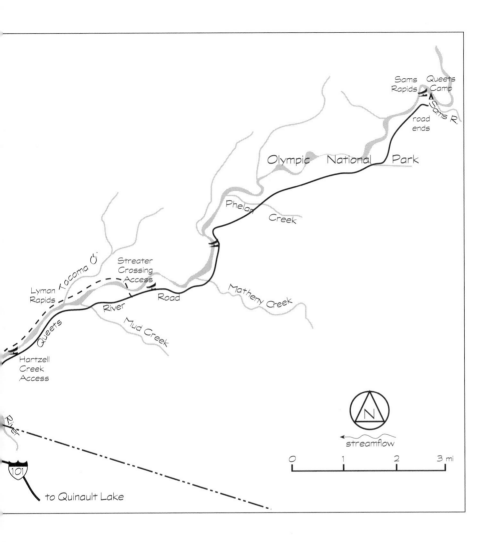

steelhead. This may be because days, or even weeks, can pass between hook-ups. When a hooked fish starts dancing across the surface, I can hardly contain myself, even when it's someone else's fish!

After a lengthy battle, with several near grabs close to shore, a 15-pound native buck came to hand. We admired, photographed, and released him back into the current to continue his spawning journey.

It is legal to keep native fish in this part of the Queets, just as it is in many Olympic Peninsula rivers, but I believe we should release all native fish unharmed. Native steelhead runs are dwindling for a variety of reasons that are beyond our individual control. Simply releasing wild steelhead is one thing we can all do to help ensure their survival.

A few weeks later, Tim and I and a couple other friends got together for our annual steelhead camp. For the past several years, Tim and I have built steelhead camp at Queets Campground. We invite all sorts of people to the event; usually two or three guys show up. Depending on river conditions, we float the Queets, or use our camp as a base for fishing smaller rivers in the area.

Steelhead camp is a sight to behold. First, we stretch a tarp about the size of a football field between a bunch of trees to keep everything dry. Then up goes the 18' by 20' outfitters tent. Tim brings all the gear for our tent/hotel, which includes (but is by no means limited to) spring mattresses, propane stove and barbecue, dining table and chairs, food storage and preparation table, coolers, portable CD stereo, a 55-gallon barrel wood stove, and wall-to-wall deck carpeting. (Sometimes it's hard to leave camp in the morning!)

There are three established boat ramps on the park stretch of the Queets. The first after leaving Highway 101 is Hartzell Creek, then comes Streater Crossing, and third is the campground. Each drift is approximately five miles long—the perfect length for a full day of winter steelheading.

One year, we decided to float the entire distance from camp to the Queets/Clearwater bridge. Our plan was to take three days to do a leisurely float, covering the water thoroughly and fishing until dark each day. We would then pull our inflatables to shore, hike up to the road which parallels the river, walk to our car (we would place a car at the appropriate boat ramp each day), and drive back to camp. The next morning we would simply return to where we'd stashed the boats and resume our float.

On the first day, we stopped to fish a riffle just as the sun disappeared in the west. When darkness swallowed us, we found ourselves along a straight, slow stretch of river. It was a beautiful evening, and since we were on a flat, very calm section of stream, we decided to continue on to the tailout of the slow stretch, which would place us closer to the road.

We drifted in utter silence. The stars were shining bright, and we could just make out the silhouettes of trees along the shoreline. Life is good, I was thinking. Then all of a sudden, the water exploded all around us. I thought the world was coming to an end! It took a while to realize what had happened; we'd floated right into a herd of elk standing in the middle of the river. So much for night floats!

A very healthy run of hatchery steelhead passes through the Queets on its way to the Salmon River. The Salmon enters the Queets just below the Hartzell Creek boat launch. The drift from Hartzell to the Queets/Clearwater bridge in early winter takes advantage of these returning fish and is very popular. The Salmon River itself flows mostly within the boundaries of the Quinault Indian Reservation and is under special regulations. (For tribal permits and regulations, contact the Quinault Indian Nation, 360-276-8211.)

The larger, native fish follow the Salmon River run, and the months of January, February, and March can offer red-hot fishing for them. In fact, the largest steelhead I've ever seen outside of northern B.C. came from the Queets River in March. On a float of the lower drift one chilly afternoon, I came across an angler who was posing with a huge steelhead which he had just taken on a Corkie and sandshrimp combination. I pulled over and photographed the fish myself. He never did get it officially weighed, but it bottomed out a pocket scale calibrated to 28 pounds, and we guessed it was easily pushing 30!

One advantage to fishing the Olympic Peninsula is that there are always options. When conditions are right, the Queets is often my first choice for steelheading. If heavy rains make the Queets unfishable, there is the Salmon River (tribal permit required), the Quinault and Humptulips rivers to the south, and a host of other steelhead

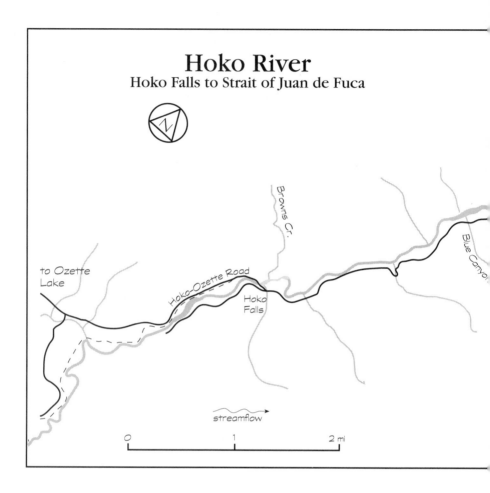

Hoko River
Hoko Falls to Strait of Juan de Fuca

Browns Cr.

Blue Canyon

to Ozette
Lake

Hoko-Ozette Road

Hoko
Falls

streamflow

0   1   2 mi

streams to the north. Except during major winter storms, there is al-most always fishable water somewhere on the Olympic Peninsula.

Since most of the fishable section of the Queets lies within the boundaries of Olympic National Park, a good source for conditions and information is the National Park Service (360-452-4501).

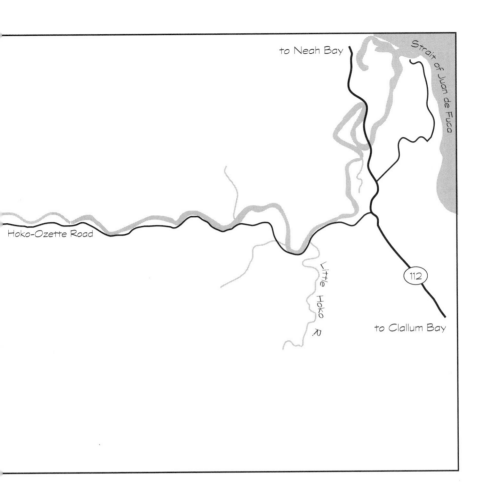

Hoko River, mid-December

When you plan a winter steelhead trip to the Olympic Peninsula a month in advance, and when the date rolls around and you find clear skies and a forecast of "no rain for the next five days," you are one lucky angler. I was just that lucky on my first trip to the Hoko River.

Unfortunately, luck didn't seem to extend to the fishing. Mory Meek and I pounded the water for nearly three hours without even a bump. I had at least a dozen favorite fly patterns stuck in the fleece patch on my vest—evidence of my futile efforts. Ever optimistic, though, we continued downstream to a hole we had worked earlier in the day. There we found two fishermen gathering gear, getting ready to leave. Both were using bait-casting rods. I noticed one fellow was using egg clusters for bait, and the other was using a spoon. One of the fellows said, "There's a fish in there, but we can't get him to take hold!" With that, they headed up the trail and out of sight.

Mory and I were just about ready to admit a "skunk," too, which certainly wouldn't be the first while winter steelheading. But we decided to try this one last hole before calling it quits. I walked to the head of the drift, cast out, and let my fly swing with the current. My sink-tip line was only halfway through its swing when it came taut.

The steelhead raced downstream to the tail of the pool, then back to the head of the pool, and then tore up the water between. Eventually, a 10-pound steelhead came to hand—a nice way to end the day.

Why did I hook a fish on fly gear when bait and gear fishermen failed? Well, to say for certain would be foolish, but the water was low and clear—conditions that make steelhead easily put off by large lures and big gobs of bait. Mory and I were using size 8 sparsely tied, low-water steelhead patterns on light, six-pound tippet—gear that is not as likely to put off the fish.

Over the years, I have found that during times of low, clear water, it really pays to size down my gear. And when it comes to sizing down their tackle, many gear fishermen don't have the right stuff. When fishing small streams for steelhead, if you are to be consistently successful, you must be prepared for low, clear conditions.

Mark Miller, a fishing pal from Raymond, is one of the best steelhead fishermen I know. He prefers to fish with jigs. When the water is low and clear I have seen him take fish when nobody else can. His secret? Six-pound leader, and a size 10 jig.

The Hoko is a relatively short stream. From its headwaters in the Olympic foothills, it travels only a short distance before spilling into the Strait of Juan de Fuca. The lower portion of this river is slow and winding, with numerous runs and pockets. Nearly the whole river is "steelhead water" and very fishable. The upper section reminds me of a mountain stream. The water is fast and shallow, very clear, with numerous pockets and pools—ideal for fly fishing. In fact, the upper portion of the river above the bridge crossing is fly-fishing-only water.

Unless you live in Forks or some of the other towns on the Olympic Peninsula, the Hoko is a long drive from just about everywhere. To get there you head for Clallam Bay, go past Sekiu a couple of miles, then hang a left on the Ozette Lake road.

A good road follows the Hoko for the first several miles to the bridge crossing. Access on the lower stretches is good, with several places to pull over and park. Access to the upper river is by foot only. If you don't mind hoofing it and like absolute solitude and fly fishing, the fly-only water is a real treat.

December and January seem to be the most productive months on the Hoko. Even so, we're not talking numbers of fish like you'll find in the larger Olympic streams. But with the Hoko, you can build a satisfying intimacy that larger rivers can't offer.

Other small steelhead streams in the Hoko vicinity worth checking out are the Pysht and the Lyre.

Quinault River, early January

The upper Quinault River is a clear, rushing mountain stream. From the bridge looking down, you can see just about every rock on the bottom of the river. It certainly doesn't look like a coastal stream, and it's very different from the

lower river that empties out of Lake Quinault. Unless there has been a horrendous storm, the Upper Quinault will usually be clear when other rivers are not fishable. It's my ace-in-the-hole on the lower Olympic Peninsula. When driving north from my home in Raymond, I look over the bridge to see if the Humptulips River is dirty. If it is, I usually head for the Quinault.

To reach the upper Quinault, take the South Shore Road off Highway 101, following it past the end of the lake. The road winds through farmland before approaching the river again. Colonel Bob and other spectacular peaks tower on the Quinault Ridge to the right. In just a few miles, you'll come to the bridge that crosses the river. Most drifters start their float here.

The biggest problem with floating this river is its ever changing channel. Seldom have I been able to use the same take-out point two seasons in a row. Hiking and wading are more predictable. Check with the Olympic National Park (360-452-4501) for conditions and current regulations.

The lower Quinault River is quite different, emerald in color and much deeper than the upper river. The lower river is seldom unfishable, though you need a tribal permit and guide since the river below the lake flows through the Quinault Reservation. A fishing permit and guide information is available at the store in Amanda Park. Permits and information are also available from the Quinault Indian Nation (360-276-8211).

Little Coastal Streams, mid-January

My son Jordan, Mark Miller, and I parked along the highway and followed the frozen muddy trail down to the river. Ice crystals in the mud crunched underfoot. Leafless alder trees along the stream blocked the rising sun—which was good for fishing but made for cold fingers. This was Jordan's first steelhead trip.

Little coastal streams can be very productive for winter steelhead.

We worked our way downstream, drifting jigs through every pocket and riffle. After an hour without so much as a bump, Jordan was at least getting the hang of drifting his jig, watching his float, and reading steelhead water. Mark, a kind man, took Jordan under his wing and gave him a crash-course on steelheading as we moved toward the gorge.

As we entered the canyon, we were joined by another friend, Bruce Mallory, who knows this little coastal stream better than anyone I know. He once had a 14-fish day here, a remarkable feat. So it wasn't surprising that Bruce hooked into a fish only moments after his arrival. I watched from downstream as Jordan ran up to take in the action. Bruce handed his rod to Jordan and let him play the steelhead. When Jordan rejoined me, he was grinning from ear to ear.

Continuing our journey down the gorge, Mark and Jordan were fishing a stretch below a small falls when Jordan yelled out that he had a fish on. The battle only lasted a few head shakes before the fish spit the jig.

A couple of holes later, I hooked a fish. Jordan played and landed that fish too, and I released the five-pound hatchery hen back into the icy water.

In the very next hole, Jordan and Bruce were drifting their jigs out in mid-river when Jordan hooked another steelhead. This one stayed on and was obviously a big fish. A lengthy battle finally brought it close. It was a native buck of around 14 pounds. I was proud when Jordan made the call to release it, even though this was his first hooked and played-out steelhead.

The final count of the day was seven steelhead. Jordan had played four of them. Not bad for a first steelhead trip, though of course, he got the impression that catching steelhead is no big deal. Boy, does he have a lot to learn!

On peril of being stoned by Jordan, Mark, and Bruce, I must refrain from telling you the name of this stream. But, the point of this story is that little streams as productive as this one can be found all along the Washington coast, uncrowded and waiting for adventurous anglers. My own favorites are simply those closest to my home in southwest Washington, including the Nemah, Naselle, Grays, Elochoman, Palix, and Willapa Rivers. (One of these, by the way, is the stream mentioned above. Guess which one!)

To find your very own steelhead stream, get at a good map of the coast and a copy of the WDFW *Sport Fishing Rules*. On the map, identify a stream with salt access, then check the rule book to see if it's listed. Only listed streams have a steelhead season. Another great source of information is the WDFW *Steelhead Update and Sport Harvest Report*. This report lists all the steelhead streams in the state and gives catch statistics compiled from the return of steelhead punch cards. It is available free of charge by calling the Department (360-902-2700).

Trout and Panfish
for the Hardy

Potholes Reservoir, late December

It had already been snowing for an hour when we began inflating our float tubes. By the time we got all of our gear assembled, there were a good three inches on the ground. Slipping into the near freezing water was awkward but tolerable thanks to multiple layers of cold-weather clothing under our waders. The occasion was our annual winter lake trip.

For a few hours we enjoyed the novelty of lake fishing for trout under the most improbable conditions. By late afternoon, the temperature dropped considerably, and we had to use our tubes as ice breakers to make it back the last ten feet to shore. We left the lake chilly, but content.

If the above image "leaves you cold," you might want to skip this chapter. But if you occasionally get unseasonable urges to pursue trout and panfish weather be damned (no need to raise your hand; you know who you are), be assured that Washington offers opportunities for winter lake fishing on both sides of the Cascade Mountains. As you plan your trips, remember that eastside lakes experience more severe weather (as in the above reminiscence) and are more frequently unfishable due to ice-over or extreme cold.

Silver Lake, mid-March

First it would rain, then hail, then the wind would howl so hard we couldn't keep the little boat under control. The calendar said it was mid-March, but for all intents and purposes, it was still February. Pinky Freeman and I were on southwest Washington's Silver Lake. We managed to find ourselves a school of crappie, and by trolling a little yellow streamer fly through a small channel on the east end of the lake, we were catching a decent fish on every pass. Trolling (never my first choice) was our only option because of the wind.

Crappie school-up during the winter, which is when I've had my best luck on Silver Lake. Yellow or white jigs and flies are what I most often use, but small spinners and bait are also effective.

Due to generally mild westside winter temperatures, almost any "nice" winter day is suitable for pursuing trout or panfish. Even the not-so-nice days (like the one described above) are fishable if you don't mind the elements.

Silver Lake and Coldwater Lake are both just off Hwy. 504, so I often fish both when I'm in the area, if there is open water at Coldwater. Remember that Coldwater is classified as a selective fishery, restricted to fly fishing. Most people who fish it in the "off season" use Woolly Buggers or similar flies fished very slowly along the bottom.

Throughout western Washington there are dozens of lakes open to winter fishing for trout and panfish. And though fishing may be considerably slower than in other seasons, you will never feel crowded on the water at this time of year!

Negotiating the Queets River in a personal boat.

Mark Miller with a low-water winter steelhead

Winter steelhead from a small Southwest Washington stream.

Many Washington lakes are open and productive in winter.

Schooling Silver Lake crappie can be taken on a small, trolled streamer.

Quail Lake, late December

It is not advisable to make long range plans for a trout or panfish trip to eastern Washington in winter. The weather is just too unpredictable. However, there are always periods when a trip can be both possible and productive.

One gray winter morning, Ron Meek and I found ourselves with an itch to fish for trout in central Washington. It had simply been too long since our last trout adventure. We focused our attention on the seep lakes and selected Quail Lake as our destination.

The sun tried valiantly to burn through the fog, which was brought on by unseasonably warm temperatures in the low 50s. But by mid-afternoon we knew it wasn't going to happen. The wind was calm, though, and the damp, tawny grasses looked especially fetching in their monochrome setting. It reminded me of a black and white photo where only one object is artificially colored.

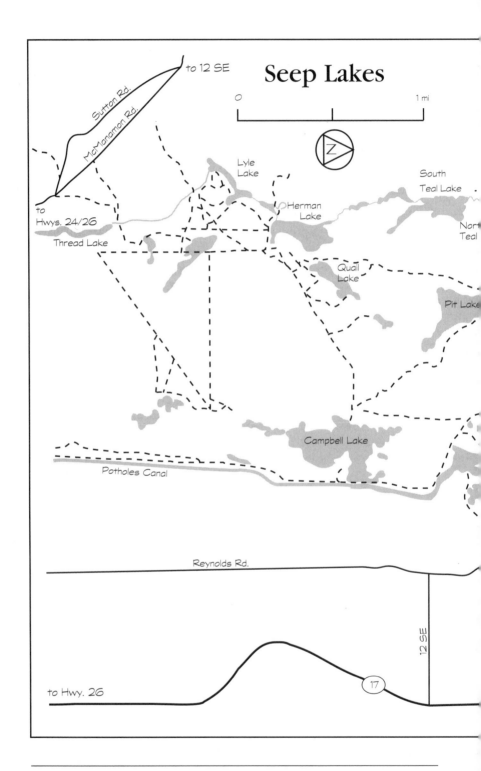

Seep Lakes

to 12 SE

Sutton Rd.
McManamon Rd.

0   1 mi

Lyle
Lake

South
Teal Lake

to
Hwys. 24/26

Herman
Lake

Nor
Teal

Thread Lake

Quail
Lake

Pit Lake

Campbell Lake

Potholes Canal

Reynolds Rd.

12 SE

to Hwy. 26

17

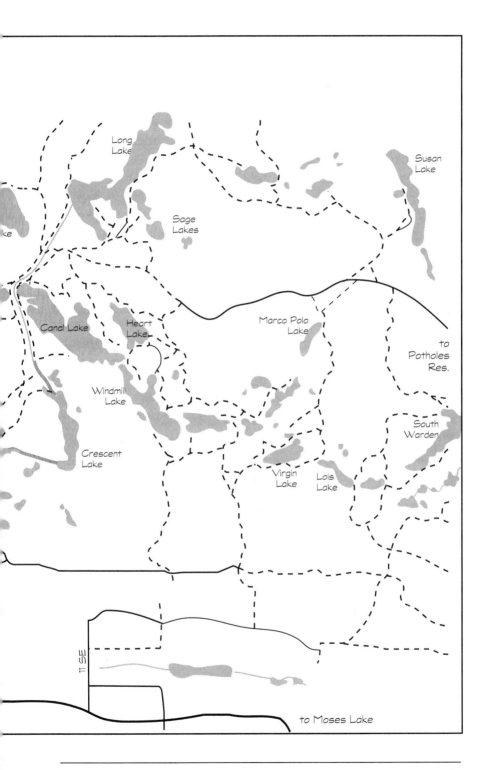

Long
Lake

Susan
Lake

Sage
Lakes

Canal Lake

Heart
Lake

Marco Polo
Lake

to
Potholes
Res.

Windmill
Lake

South
Warden

Crescent
Lake

Virgin
Lake

Lois
Lake

11 SE

to Moses Lake

As we approached a stand of dead reeds near the west end of the lake, we jumped a couple of snoozing mallards, momentarily scaring the wits out of all four of us. While regaining my composure, I studied the lake and noticed a dimple on the water, then another, and another. Close observation revealed a hatch of midges, and the trout were taking good advantage of the treat.

The pupal cases floating in the water were darkish in color, so we selected similar imitations, tying size 16 midge pupae to finely tapered tippets. We slipped our tubes into the water, and for the next few hours enjoyed some of the best winter trout fishing either of us had ever experienced. Several rainbows to 20 inches came to the net while the brief afternoon hatch lasted.

The best time to be on the water for winter trout is during the "heat of the day" (around 2 p.m.). This is when aquatic insects (and consequently trout) are most active. As for hatches, about the only thing you can expect to find on these lakes is midges, which hatch all year as long as there is ice-free water.

Winter trouting in Washington's lakes isn't always fast and easy. In fact, most of the time it is considerably slower than in other seasons. Fish metabolisms are down when the water is cold, and they don't need to eat as much as when the water is warmer.

Quail Lake is a fly-fishing-only lake, but in the immediate area there are nearly 40 other unrestricted lakes open to year 'round fishing. For information as to which lakes are open and "hot," call Mar Don Resort (509-346-2651). Occasionally, during severe winters, some of these relatively shallow lakes freeze solidly enough to offer safe ice fishing opportunities. The folks at Mar Don Resort will be able to advise you.

Resident Salmon

South Puget Sound, early December

The tide was slack, and the water was as calm and flat as could be. That made it easy to cast while standing in the little flat-bottomed boat. My dad and I were fishing in North Bay, near Allyn, in South Puget Sound. (South Puget Sound is generally considered to be those marine waters from the Tacoma Narrows south to Olympia and Shelton.) We had worked our way into a shallow cove with a gravel beach and were casting small baitfish patterns towards the shore, stripping them back in an erratic fashion, trying to emulate the frantic movements of a baitfish with a salmon hot on its tail.

There was a nip in the air, and the gray overcast (nature's own polarizer) made visibility into the water sharp enough that we could see rocks and shells on the bottom.

The first salmon I caught, a resident coho no bigger than a good eastside trout, was vigorous and acrobatic, leaping and cartwheeling around the boat. My 7-weight fly rod was entirely adequate for the battle.

Working our way around the cove, we caught and released a dozen or so silvers before calling it quits.

Although migrating salmon have been declining for the past several years throughout the northwest, Puget Sound hosts a healthy population of non-migrating salmon that provide good winter angling. These residents, both coho and chinook (known locally as silvers and blackmouths respectively), begin their lives in WDFW hatcheries. Through a variety of methods (including net holding pens scattered throughout the Sound south of Seattle) these salmon are encouraged to remain in the Sound throughout their lifetimes.

While blackmouth tend to swim deep, coho travel at relatively shallow depths, so fly fishing for them is especially effective and increasingly popular. Most fly anglers use 6- or 7-weight rods, and sink-tip or full-sinking lines. When fish are visibly working the surface, I prefer an intermediate sinking line simply because it's easier to pick up off the water and cast all day long. Full-floating lines will also work when fish are on the top, which is fairly often in the case of coho.

Silvers are aggressive feeders in this environment, so a variety of flies can be effective. I prefer baitfish patterns in sizes 4 and 6. Other anglers use tube flies or flashy steelhead flies like the Comet and Flash Fly.

Spinning outfits also take a lot of coho here. I generally use a medium weight spinning rod, casting quarter-ounce hammered brass spoons.

Resident coho are schooling fish, and their presence at various locations throughout the south Sound can be somewhat predictable. Nevertheless, it's always good to get a fishing report from someone near the water who talks to anglers every day. For information about fishing in the Tacoma area, call the Narrows Marina (206-564-4222) and the Morning Hatch Fly Shoppe (206-472-1070). For information about the Olympia area, call George Beech at The Fly Fisher (360-491-0181).

One of the best spots for blackmouth in the south Sound is Lyle Point, at the south end of Anderson Island. Moochers and trollers work the banks here with herring, and at times do quite well.

Other blackmouth hot spots in the South Sound include Eagle Island (between Anderson and McNeil Islands), the southern shore of Fox Island, and Devil's Head (the south end of the Key Peninsula). There are, of course, other areas that also produce well. To find blackmouth, ask at the marinas, and don't be shy about watching other boats.

There are a number of boat ramps in the South Sound area, including the Narrows Marina in Tacoma (just south of the Narrows Bridge), Luhr Beach (on the west end of Nisqually Flats), and Boston Harbor (north of Olympia).

Nautical charts for this area are available at most marinas and at many sporting goods stores. You can also find them at Captain's Nautical Supply (206-283-7242).

Central Puget Sound, late December

With the Seattle metropolitan area bursting at its doorstep, central Puget Sound probably gets more fishing pressure than any saltwater in the Northwest. Though winter thins out the crowd somewhat, many anglers take  advantage of the excellent salmon fishing opportunities here.

The primary target species is blackmouth (resident chinook), which are fished around the dozens of headlands and fingers of land that jut into the Sound. Two of my favorite blackmouth fisheries are at Possession Bar (South Whidbey Island) and Jefferson Point (known locally as "Jeff Head"). Other popular spots are the northern tip of Vashon Island and the east side of Bainbridge Island. There are many other productive areas besides these.

One winter the blackmouth fishing at Jeff Head was particularly hot. Since it was an especially pleasant, calm day—and since Jeff Head is only five miles from downtown Seattle—I was not alone. The Sound was thick with watercraft of every kind, from cartoppers on up.

Since blackmouth are usually found at 15 to 30 fathoms (90-180 feet), trolling with downriggers and plug-cut herring, Hoochies, or plugs is the routine. (Some anglers add a dodger 18 to 48 inches above the bait when using a squid outfit.)

On this day, anglers who got down deep enough caught blackmouth. Those who didn't took the occasional coho. In our boat, where we were all fly fishing, we caught nothing! Which isn't to say you can't fly fish for blackmouth. Getting down to their level is the key. Successful blackmouth fly anglers use fast, full-sinking lines (Type 5 or 6) with baitfish imitations.

To find good coho and blackmouth fishing in the Central Sound area, contact the local marinas to see what's going on. A few (of many) on the Central Sound are Salmon Bay Tackle in Seattle (206-789-4335), Point Defiance Boat House in Tacoma (206-591-5325), and Kitsap Sport Shop in Bremerton (360-373-9589). You might also want to do a bit of exploring yourself. Pick up a chart for the Sound or use Delorme's *Washington Atlas and Gazeteer* to identify likely points near boat ramps. Look for concentrations of birds (frequently a sign that bait fish are in the area) or other fishing boats (also a reliable sign!).

North Puget Sound, late December

North Puget Sound (north of Whidbey Island) is the gateway for migrating salmon, which have long been the focus of most salmon angling here. However, as those stocks have declined, local anglers have turned to resident salmon as elsewhere throughout the Sound.

North Puget Sound is big and complex, with fishing opportunities limited only by the size of your boat and by weather and water conditions. Tide plays a major role in the feeding habits of all saltwater fish, including Puget Sound salmon. Among other things, the tide dictates where baitfish and other food can be found. Different tidal conditions seem to trigger salmon feeding (and consequent angling success). Slack water on the tide turn (either high or low) is usually unproductive. Two hours before and two hours after the tide turn are consistently the most productive times for fishing.

Tying the Saltwater Baitfish

Hook: Mustad 34011 size 2/0

Thread: White monocord

Tail: Golden pheasant neck

Body: Silver braid

Beard: Pearl Lite Brite

Eyes: Pearl stick-on type

Wing: White SLF Hanks, then pearl Krystal Flash, then silver Flashabou, then peacock Angel Hair.

Step 1: Take two of the green neck feathers from a golden pheasant skin and place dull sides together. Secure to hook forming the tail.

Step 2: Tie in a piece of silver braid and wind on the body.

Step 3: For the wing, tie in a small bunch of white SLF, then pearl Krystal Flash, then silver Flashabou, then peacock Angel Hair. Trim to length of tail.

Step 4: Tie in a beard of pearl Lite Brite.

Step 5: Wind on a large head and place a pearl-colored stick-on eye to each side.

Step 6: Whip finish head and cover with five-minute clear epoxy.

There are exceptions, however. At times there is a tremendous bite right at flood tide, while extreme tides often create strong currents that scatter both baitfish and their predators.

Keep in mind, too, that extreme tides combined with wind can create hazardous boating conditions. Keep safety in mind at all times, and be prepared to make a quick exit if need be.

For smaller craft, the Whidbey Island area is usually a productive, safe bet. Salmon fishing has historically been good along western Whidbey Island north to Deception Pass. Admiralty Head (at Fort Casey, about midway up the west coast of the island) offers particularly good blackmouth fishing. South Whidbey's prominent points of land are also frequently productive, with Bush Point the most popular. Boat ramps convenient to these fisheries include Fort Casey and Bush Point, as well as Port Townsend on the Olympic Peninsula directly across the Sound from Admiralty Head.

Local information goes a long way. For information about fishing the west side of Whidbey Island from Partridge Point to Bush Point, call Fish 'n' Hole in Port Townsend (360-385-7031). Vehicle access to Whidbey Island is by way of Hwy. 20 west from Burlington or by ferry from Mukilteo or Port Townsend.

Whitefish

Viewed as trash by many anglers, the lowly whitefish gets little respect in the Pacific Northwest throughout most of the year. I don't know why this is so. It's often hard to tell the fight of a hefty whitefish from that of a rainbow trout of the same size. Nevertheless, I've watched countless anglers excitedly hook and play a hot fish, only to discover, several minutes into the battle, that it's a whitefish. They immediately lose all enthusiasm and horse the fish in.

In winter, however, with trout lying low for the most part, whitefish gain some respectability and even have a devoted following.

As a 10-year old kid hanging out in the local sporting goods store on winter Saturdays, I would often hear an old guy bragging about whitefish conquests on the Yakima. I wasn't allowed near the river at that age, but I remember looking forward to the prospect in the same way an adult angler might look forward to fishing Alaska!

The years flew by, and eventually whitefish found their way into my creel. Alaska did, too, in a manner of speaking. But that's another story.

Yakima River, mid-January

It was bright, but the sun held little warmth as I walked down to the river with Don Eckis, an old school pal. The dry, powdery snow crunched but didn't pack under our feet. Each breath was fresh and exhilarating, and it hurt if you  breathed too deeply. Air temperature was probably about 20°F.

When we reached the river, we saw sparkling silver slashes in a long flat below the riffle. Whitefish. In summer whitefish are dispersed throughout the river, but in winter they school up in tailouts and stretches of moderate flow. Once you locate a school, you can often fish it all day in the same spot, since whitefish don't spook easily.

A few other anglers were already fishing the flat, and there were several frozen whitefish scattered in the snow behind them. As we watched, one of the fellows yanked in another fish, quickly unhooked it, and gave it a quick toss over with the others.

I asked the guy what he was using, though I had already made a guess. "A size 12 whitefish fly, topped off with a maggot," was his reply. I knew this was the standard for regulars on the Yakima; by this time I was tying flies for the local sporting goods store, and I remember thinking some of these guys might be using flies from my vise.

A whitefish fly is a simple tie: a floss body (in red, yellow, white, brown, or green) with brown hackle wound over the top. It looks a lot like a small Woolly Worm. Some feel the maggot is essential, but I never used one. These days, in fact, I generally use caddis larvae or mayfly nymph imitations. Now that I know that's what the whitefish are eating, it only makes sense. But whitefish flies worked just fine.

The tactic is simple, too. Place enough weight on the line (a foot or so above the fly) to keep it on the bottom, then cast to a likely spot or, better yet, to one where you see whitefish sparkling. Dead-drift through, keeping all slack out of the line and setting the hook at the least hesitation in the drift. This method works for both spinning and fly gear.

Of all the whitefish days that followed, I remember this one best. Perhaps because we caught so many of the tasty smokers—some up to 18 inches—fishing till our feet grew numb from the cold.

On the Yakima, whitefish are generally available in all the usual trout hangouts from Cle Elum through the Yakima Canyon. It's easy to find seclusion, too, at this time of year. Just drive the old road from Ellensburg to Cle Elem, or the Canyon Road south of Ellensburg. Pull over at any wide spot, and walk down to the water. Chances are, you'll have the day—and the whitefish—all to yourself.

Whitefish are found in many eastside streams, including tributaries of the Yakima River, such as the Naches, Tieton, and Cle Elum rivers. To the north and east, you'll find whitefish in the Wenatchee and Kettle Rivers.

Upper Quinault River, late January

The temperature hovered around 20 degrees Fahrenheit, cold for these parts. High pressure dominated the whole state, and western Washington was caught in one of its rare (twice-a-winter) freeze-ups. Though cold, the day was sunny, too sunny for steelhead, and the river was too low. But since we'd made the two-hour drive to the Quinault, we didn't think of turning back.

Terry Lewis, Mory Meek, and I were slipping and sliding as we negotiated the ice-covered rocks at the river's edge to launch the drift boat. The sky was as blue as blue. Along the banks of the river, leafless alders stood sentry for the regiments of fir and hemlock beyond.

There were three of us in the driftboat. Two would fish while the other rowed. After a while, we'd switch off so everyone would get a chance to fish. But the rower never seemed anxious to trade-off. We weren't catching any fish, and the oarsman had the best view (and was staying warm, too, the sneaky devil) as we floated leisurely through the sparkling day.

About three hours into our float, we pulled over for lunch. As I sat eating cold chicken and sipping a micro brew, I saw a flash in the river near the beached boat. I knew what it was.

I didn't have any small flies with me on this trip; my winter steelhead patterns are all pretty big. But I tied on my smallest fly, a sandshrimp pattern tied on a size 4 hook; still too big, but I wanted to give it a shot. All my previous experience with whitefish had been on size 12 or 14 hooks.

I clamped a big split-shot to my tippet about a foot from the fly and cast out into the run where I could still see flashing fish. I must say, I was a bit surprised when my drift stopped short. A scrappy battle produced a chunky 14-inch whitefish, the oversized shrimp fly stuck fast in it's lower jaw. Over the course of the next hour, we took a dozen whitefish out of this one hole and had a ball.

Until that day, I didn't realize there were whitefish in Washington's coastal rivers. But subsequently, I have fished for them successfully in the Queets and the Hoh. My guess is that they can be found in nearly all coastal streams of any size.

Final Thoughts

When summer gets too long and hot for me, with temperatures soaring, I find myself dreaming of the fall, ready for cooler days and for the first hard autumn rains that bring the salmon home. Then someone will hook the first steelhead of the winter, and I'll find myself chasing anadramous rainbows all over the coast. Though after a couple months of frozen guides and numb fingers, my mind drifts off to spring, and trout.

Spring will fly by; it always does. But summer will open up all sorts of possibilities: casting flies to rockfish and lingcod, getting into the high mountain lakes as soon as the trails are free of snow, and summer steelhead will be fun. Until it gets too hot for me.

And then I'll dream again of fall.

Directory of Resources and Services
(fishery in italics)

Barrier Dam Campground, *Cowlitz River*	360-985-2495
Big Salmon Resort, *Neah Bay, north Coast*	360-645-2374
Blue Creek Bait & Tackle, *Cowlitz River*	360-864-6015
Captain's Nautical Supplies, *maps, charts*	206-283-7242
Clallum Bay-Sekiu C. of C., *north coast*	360-963-2339
Coldwater Ridge Visitor Center, *Coldwater & Castle lakes*	360-274-2131
Cooper's Fly Shop, *Yakima River*	509-962-5259
Davis, Skip, Guide Service, *Potholes Res.*	509-349-8004
Fish 'n' Hole, *Puget Sound, north*	360-385-7031
Herb's Motel & Charters, *Neah Bay*	360-963-2346
Hoh River Resort, *Hoh River*	360-374-5566
Kitsap Sport Shop, *Puget Sound, central*	360-373-9589
Lewis River Sports, *Lewis River*	360-225-9530
Long Beach C. of C., *Long Beach lakes*	360-642-2400
Mar Don Resort, *Potholes Reservoir*	509-349-8004
Morning Hatch, *Puget Sound, central*	206-472-1070
Narrows Marina, *Puget Sound*	206-564-4222
Olson's Resort & Charters, *Neah Bay*	360-963-2311
Olympic National Park, *Olympics*	360-452-4501
Olympic Sporting Goods, *Olympics*	360-374-6330
Pt. Defiance Boat House, *Puget Sound*	206-591-5325
Prichard's Western Angler, *Kalama River*	360-673-4690
Quinault Indian Nation, *Queets & Quinault*	360-276-8211
Salmon Bay Tackle, *Puget Sound*	206-789-4335
Evening Hatch Fly Shop, *Yakima River*	509-574-8334
The Fly Fisher, *Puget Sound, south*	360-491-0181
WDFW Fish Management	360-902-2700
WDFW Poaching Hot Line	800-477-6224
WDFW Sport Fishing Hot Line	206-976-3200
Wenatchee National Forest, *Alpine Lakes*	509-674-4411
Westport C. of C., *Half-Moon Bay*	360-268-9422
Westward Hoh Resort, *Hoh River*	360-374-6657